INTRODUCTION TO
THE LAW OF THE
ARAMAIC PAPYRI

Oxford University Press, Amen House, London E.C.4

GLASGOW NEW YORK TORONTO MELBOURNE WELLINGTON
BOMBAY CALCUTTA MADRAS KARACHI LAHORE DACCA
CAPE TOWN SALISBURY NAIROBI IBADAN ACCRA
KUALA LUMPUR HONG KONG

INTRODUCTION TO
THE LAW OF THE ARAMAIC PAPYRI

BY

REUVEN YARON, D.Phil.

Lecturer in Roman Law
in the Hebrew University, Jerusalem

OXFORD
AT THE CLARENDON PRESS
1961

TO
DAVID DAUBE

PREFACE

THIS *Introduction to the Law of the Aramaic Papyri* is addressed primarily to the reader who, while interested in legal history and ancient law, has no knowledge of Semitic languages. In writing it, I have endeavoured to follow the example set by introductory books, such as those of Seidl, on ancient Egyptian law,[1] and of Steinwenter, on the law of the Coptic documents.[2] Like these two authors, I had only rather limited material at my disposal; hence my suggestions and conclusions will not infrequently involve some measure of uncertainty.

Legal historical research has so far taken little notice of the Aramaic papyri, mainly, I presume, because of difficulties of language, a feature which—at least to some extent—they have in common with the ancient Egyptian and Coptic material. Scholars are wary—very rightly so—of using sources which they are not able to read in the original. Much work and ingenuity have indeed been devoted to translating these documents and interpreting them, but this was mainly done by non-lawyers, and the lawyer will not always be satisfied with what he is offered. Unable to apply his own mind independently to the question, he will prefer to exclude the Aramaic documents altogether from the orbit of his research, just as he will the sources written in Accadian and Egyptian, to mention only the two most important of many. Here lies one of the reasons for the concentration of legal historical research on Roman law, and, though to a considerably lesser extent, on the material preserved in Greek. Yet, while legal historians are understandably anxious to avoid possible sources of error, the disregard of such substantial parts of ancient law is itself bound to produce in them a particularistic attitude to many of its phenomena and thereby lead to mistakes.

'Ancient law' is a general term, which covers all the various

---

[1] *Einführung in die ägyptische Rechtsgeschichte bis zum Ende des Neuen Reiches*, 2nd ed., 1951; *Ägyptische Rechtsgeschichte der Saiten- und Perserzeit*, 1956.
[2] *Das Recht der koptischen Urkunden*, 1955.

legal systems of antiquity. There is no wish to suggest that there ever existed an ancient common law, that is to say, a set of rules derived from one ultimate source, and applied—subject to local variations—throughout the ancient world. It was, indeed, a world split and divided into ethnical and political units, differing *lingua, institutis, legibus*. On the other hand, the peoples and states of antiquity were not without contact with each other; there was from early times considerable exchange, not only of material products, but also of cultural, religious, and legal notions. Even where there was no contact, similarity in economic and social conditions often brought about a similar approach to problems demanding attention and solution. It is therefore often legitimate to rely, for example, for the interpretation of a rule of Roman law, on comparable rules in other ancient systems, even if greatly distant in space and time. (Only in doing so one ought to forgo speaking of 'influence', except in those cases where an examination of the circumstances tends to prove its existence.) Actually, it is arguable that for a proper under-standing of any given ancient legal system it is necessary to have regard also to the others. To be sure, no one can hope to be expert in all of them, yet every legal historian should wish to obtain a bird's-eye view of ancient law, as the sum total of a considerable number of different, more or less independent systems. It is the aim of this book to supply one section of this legal panorama.

Introductions are exposed to dangers inherent in their very nature. The need to avoid dealing with minute details, the need also to abstain from discussing points of language on which the true meaning of a document will often depend—may lead to superficiality and shallowness on the one hand, to bold and un-warranted generalization on the other. To avoid these pitfalls, I dealt first in detail with some central topics in a series of articles,[1] and used these as a basis for the present book. The

[1] 'The Schema of the Aramaic Legal Documents', *Journal of Semitic Studies*, ii (1957), pp. 33–61; 'Aramaic Marriage Contracts from Elephantine', ibid. iii (1958), pp. 1–39; to be read together with 'Aramaic Marriage Contracts: Corrigenda and Addenda', ibid. v (1960), pp. 66–70; 'Identities in the Brooklyn Museum Aramaic Papyri', *Biblica*, xxxix (1958), pp. 344–54; 'On Defension Clauses

results obtained in the articles have been considered anew, and
on a number of points I have changed my view (usually without
stating that fact). On the whole they have enabled me to be
here relatively brief, and yet refer the interested reader to a
more detailed examination of specific points.

In vocalizing Aramaic words I have been helped by colleagues
who are linguists. They stress that the vocalization is frequently
open to doubt. It would certainly have been simpler, safer and
more exact to adhere to the consonant spelling of the texts
themselves. However, I believe that the reader who knows no
Aramaic will find it easier to be introduced to, and keep in mind,
words with vowels than combinations of consonants, and, as
long as full accuracy is not claimed, no harm will result. As an
additional safeguard, arbitrary vocalizations have been marked
by an asterisk preceding the word. A different matter again is
transliteration. I have tried to make that as simple as possible,
even at the expense of meticulous grammatical distinction.

The manuscript has been read by Professor G. R. Driver,
Dr. Z. W. Falk, Dr. S. E. Loewenstamm, and Dr. H. B. Rosén.
To all of them my thanks are due for their observations, by
which I have benefited greatly. Dr. H. Tadmor has checked the
quotations in Accadian, Mrs. S. Groll those in Egyptian. Dr. S.
Perlman has read the proofs.

To Professor David Daube, the scholar and the man, this
little book is dedicated in gratitude and affection. In gratitude,
because of his acute criticisms of both form and substance. In
affection, because of the incomparable manner, the cheerfulness
of heart, in which his assistance was offered, on this occasion and
on many others.   R. Y.

The Hebrew University
Jerusalem, July 1961

of some Oriental Deeds of Sale and Lease, from Mesopotamia and Egypt', *Bibliotheca Orientalis*, xv (1958), pp. 15–22; 'Aramaic Deeds of Conveyance', *Biblica*, xli
(1960), pp. 248–74, 379–94; and, finally, 'Notes on Aramaic Papyri', *Revue Inter-
nationale des Droits de l'Antiquité*, v (1958), pp. 299–310; *Journal of Near Eastern Studies*,
xx (1961), pp. 127–30.

CONTENTS

ABBREVIATIONS

AASOR	*Annual of the American Schools of Oriental Research.*
ARU	J. Kohler–A. Ungnad, *Assyrische Rechtsurkunden*, 1913.
b.	*bar*—'son of'.
C	Papyrus no. . . ., in Cowley.
CAD	*The Assyrian Dictionary*, Chicago.
'Conveyances'	R. Yaron, 'Aramaic Deeds of Conveyance', *Biblica*, xli (1960), pp. 248–74, 379–94.
Cowley	A. Cowley, *Aramaic Papyri of the 5th Century B.C.*, 1923.
'Defension Clauses'	R. Yaron, 'On Defension Clauses of some Oriental Deeds of Sale and Lease, from Mesopotamia and Egypt', *Bibliotheca Orientalis*, xv (1958), pp. 15–22.
Driver	G. R. Driver, *Aramaic Documents of the Fifth Century B.C.*, 1954.
Driver and Miles	G. R. Driver and J. Miles, *The Babylonian Laws I, Legal Commentary*, 1952.
EL	G. Eisser–J. Lewy, *Die altassyrischen Rechtsurkunden vom Kültepe*, 1930–5.
Gifts	R. Yaron, *Gifts in Contemplation of Death in Jewish and Roman Law*, 1960.
Ginsberg	H. L. Ginsberg, 'The Brooklyn Museum Aramaic Papyri', *Journal of the American Oriental Society*, lxxiv (1954), pp. 153–62.
'Identities'	R. Yaron, 'Identities in the Brooklyn Museum Aramaic Papyri', *Biblica*, xxxix (1958), pp. 344–54.
JEA	*Journal of Egyptian Archaeology.*
JNES	*Journal of Near Eastern Studies.*
JSS	*Journal of Semitic Studies.*
K	Papyrus no. . . ., in Kraeling.
KAJ	E. Ebeling, *Keilschrifttexte aus Assur juristischen Inhalts*, 1927.
Kraeling	E. G. Kraeling, *The Brooklyn Museum Aramaic Papyri*, 1953.
Kutscher	E. Y. Kutscher, 'New Aramaic Texts', *Journal of the American Oriental Society*, lxxiv (1954), pp. 233–48.

Lüddeckens	E. Lüddeckens, *Ägyptische Eheverträge*, 1960.
'Marriage Contracts'	R. Yaron, 'Aramaic Marriage Contracts from Elephantine', JSS iii (1958), pp. 1–39.
MDP	V. Scheil, *Mémoires de la délégation en Perse*, xxii (1930); xxiii (1932); xxiv (1933).
NRV	M. San Nicolò–A. Ungnad, *Neubabylonische Rechts- und Verwaltungsurkunden*, 1935.
P.	Papyrus.
Pritsch	E. Pritsch, 'Jüdische Rechtsurkunden aus Ägypten', *Zeitschrift für vergleichende Rechtswissenschaft*, xxvii (1912), pp. 7–70.
PRU	J. Nougayrol, *Le Palais royal d'Ugarit*, iii (1955); iv (1956).
Rabinowitz	J. J. Rabinowitz, *Jewish Law—Its Influence on the Development of Legal Institutions*, 1956.
RIDA	*Revue Internationale des Droits de l'Antiquité*.
'Schema'	R. Yaron, 'The Schema of the Aramaic Legal Documents', JSS ii (1957), pp. 33–61.
Seidl, *Einführung*	E. Seidl, *Einführung in die ägyptische Rechtsgeschichte bis zum Ende des Neuen Reiches*, 2nd ed., 1951.
Seidl, *Rechtsgeschichte*	E. Seidl, *Ägyptische Rechtsgeschichte der Saiten- und Perserzeit*, 1956.
UAZP	M. Schorr, *Urkunden des altbabylonischen Zivil- und Prozessrechts*, 1913.
Volterra, 'Affrancazioni'	E. Volterra, 'Le affrancazioni di schiavi nei documenti aramaici dell V secolo A. C.', *Rivista degli Studi Orientali*, xxxii (1957), pp. 675–96.
ZA	*Zeitschrift für Assyriologie*.

I

The Material

Introduction

THIS book is devoted to an examination of the legal documents in Aramaic, and the notions and rules reflected in them. All the documents but one come from the Jewish military colony in Elephantine, at the southern border of Egypt, and were written in the course of the fifth century B.C. The material at our disposal consists of approximately thirty more or less complete documents and of a considerable number of fragments. They are conveniently available in the publications of A. Cowley and E. G. Kraeling. Cowley's *Aramaic Papyri of the Fifth Century B.C.*[1] is a collection of all the Aramaic documents which were known at the time of its publication, in 1923. In 1953 Kraeling published *The Brooklyn Museum Aramaic Papyri*.[2]

The discovery of the Aramaic papyri from Elephantine at the beginning of the century aroused much interest in the scholarly world, especially because of some non-legal documents, which shed new light on questions of Jewish history and religion, but which are essentially outside the scope of the present discussion. As a matter of fact another batch of documents from Elephantine had been acquired by the American Egyptologist C. E. Wilbour early in 1893, but he died in 1896 without having disclosed his secret to anyone. It was only half a century later, in 1947, when his daughter donated the papyri to the Brooklyn Museum, that their existence became generally known.

Some details concerning the nature and origin of the colony, as well as its political, social, and religious background, are indispensable for a proper understanding of the documents. Fortunately we are able to refer to Kraeling's Historical Introduction to the Brooklyn papyri, where an excellent summary will be found of all that is known about the colony.

[1] Oxford, 1923.   [2] Yale University Press, New Haven.

There is only one other relevant papyrus, P. Meissner,[1] of 515 B.C., the provenance of which is not known, but which apparently does not come from Elephantine. It is doubtful whether either of the parties is Jewish.[2] This document, a deed of lease of a field, proves what would anyhow have been probable: that the Aramaic documents in Egypt go back to a time earlier than the fifth century, and that their use was not confined to one place only. Just how early and how widespread they were, we cannot know. Very likely they go back to the first moment of immigration of Aramaic-speaking foreigners into Egypt: for if the immigrants had once taken to having their documents drawn up in Egyptian, there would have been no reason for a subsequent switch back to the Aramaic.

Of a different character altogether are the Aramaic documents, written on leather, which have been published by G. R. Driver.[3] These are thirteen letters, instructions of an official or semi-official nature, issued by the Persian satrap of Egypt and other high-ranking Persian officers to their subordinates.[4] They have almost no connexion with private law; consequently we shall have only few occasions to refer to them.

Ordinarily the Elephantine papyri are not difficult to read. Provided a document is in a fair state of preservation, doubts will rarely arise. The only qualification to be added stems from the close similarity, perhaps even identity, of *d* and *r*. Where a word is well known from other sources there will be no problem. But if the word does not occur outside the Elephantine group the reading will be uncertain. Accordingly, it is not clear whether *regel* or *degel* is correct for the word apparently meaning 'military unit'; on the whole scholars tend to prefer the latter reading, on the strength of the Biblical *degel*—'standard'.[5] *'avigedan*—'penalty', may equally well be *'avigeran*. There is

---

[1] Published by H. Bauer and B. Meissner, *Sitzungsberichte der Preußischen Akademie der Wissenschaften*, 1936, pp. 414–24. A considerably improved edition is that of A. Dupont-Sommer in the *Mémoires de l'Académie des Inscriptions et Belles Lettres*, xiv/ii (1944), pp. 61–106.

[2] Concerning the name of the lessor, see F. Rosenthal, *Die aramaistische Forschung seit Theodor Nöldekes Veröffentlichungen*, 1939, p. 36, note 4.

[3] *Aramaic Documents of the Fifth Century B.C.*, Oxford, 1954.

[4] See Driver, p. 2.   [5] See, for example, Numbers 2. 2, 3.

no need to multiply examples. In quite a number of cases readings diverging from those of the editors have been advanced on the basis of the interchangeability of these two letters.[1] Needless to say, such new readings are not inevitably correct. All will depend on a careful examination of the context, and occasionally it will be impossible to reach certainty.

As a rule different words are clearly separated from each other. Hence mistaken division (the transfer of a letter from one word to another, the joining of two words into one, the division of one word into two), a common source of error in reading ancient manuscripts, is almost entirely avoided.[2]

Contents

According to their contents the documents can be classified as follows:

Only two documents, C 7, 16, both fragmentary, concern complaints before a court. C 49 may refer to an action for the recovery of a debt. C 44 may be a declaration on oath.

In the area of the law of persons there are three marriage contracts: C 15, K 2, 7; and two fragments relating to marriage, C 18, K 14.[3] There is one document of manumission, K 5, and one concerning adoption, K 8.

The law of property is the department best represented. By far the largest group of documents can be brought under the heading of 'conveyances', using this term in a very wide sense. Here we have deeds concerning (i) barter (C 1, 43?); (ii) sale (C 13[4], K 1, 3, 12); (iii) gift (C 8, 46, K 4, 6, 9, 10); (iv) deeds of

---

[1] e.g. in K 6: 5, 9: 4 *miṣraith*—'in Egyptian', instead of Kraeling's difficult *miṣdith* (Ginsberg, p. 161); in K 7: 7 *gammidah*, a kind of garment, instead of Kraeling's *gemirah* (G. R. Driver, *Palestine Exploration Fund Quarterly*, lxxxvii (1955), p. 93; Kutscher, p. 236); in K 11: 10 *be'arevanay*—'over my pledges', instead of Kraeling's *be'ad benay* (H. L. Ginsberg, JNES xviii (1959), pp. 148 f.); in the same line *leme<'>ḥad*—'to seize', instead of Kraeling's *limḥar*—'tomorrow' (R. Yaron, JNES xx (1961), p. 127).

[2] Actually, the only instance of this kind that comes to mind is the reading *be'ad benay* (see the preceding footnote).

[3] Insignificant fragments, to which we shall have no opportunity to refer, are C 36, 48.

[4] More exactly a case of *datio in solutum*: unable to return chattels he had obtained from his daughter, and having no money, Maḥseiah conveys to Mivṭaḥiah

submission (or 'removal'),[1] subsequent to litigation (C 6, 14, 20, 25). Only by a single document each are represented (v) provisions for the reversion of property (C 9); (vi) division of inheritance (C 28); and, finally, (vii) arrangements arising from a grant of building rights (C 5).

From obligations we have, first of all, three deeds of loan (C 10, 11, K 11), supplemented by some fragments also reflecting creditor-debtor relations (C 35, 45?, also C 49). C 2, apparently a contract relating to the haulage of corn for the garrison at Elephantine (or Syene), would be of great interest were it not in such a bad state of preservation. C 3, perhaps a duplicate of C 2, is worse. The only deed of lease is P. Meissner, providing for a crop-sharing tenancy.

Archives

Modern papyrology attaches considerable importance to the arrangement of any documents, as far as that is possible, in coherent 'archives', referring either to a particular property, or to the legal transactions of a particular person or family.[2] Two such archives can be distinguished in our material. Naming them by the person most prominent in each, we shall call them, the archives, respectively, of Mivṭaḥiah[3] and of Anani b. Azariah.

The archive of Mivṭaḥiah contains ten documents and covers a period of sixty years (471–411 B.C.). It reflects the legal activities of Mivṭaḥiah's father, Maḥseiah b. Yedoniah, of Mivṭaḥiah herself, and of her two sons Yedoniah and Maḥseiah (named after their great-grandfather and grandfather, respectively).[4] To enumerate the documents: C 5 follows from a grant of building rights made by Maḥseiah to one Koniah

---

a house (or a building-plot?) in discharge of his obligations. And see already M. San Nicolò, *Archiv Orientální*, ix (1932), p. 179.

[1] For a discussion of the pertinent Aramaic term, *reḥaq*, see pp. 81 f., below.

[2] See Seidl, *Rechtsgeschichte*, p. 11.

[3] Occasionally spelled Mifṭaḥiah.

[4] The ten documents are considered together in A. Sayce and A. Cowley, *Aramaic Papyri Discovered at Assuan*, 1906, which also contains a deed of loan, C 11, apparently not belonging to the archive of Mivṭaḥiah. Cowley, in his 1923 edition, preferred a chronological order of all the documents to preserving the archive as an entity.

b. Zadok; in C 5 the grantee undertakes not to interfere with certain rights of the grantor. C 6 is a deed of submission. Dargman b. Ḥarshin had contested Maḥseiah's title to a certain piece of land, but had lost his case; he renounces his claim. C 8 is a deed of gift: Maḥseiah donates a plot of a house to Miv-ṭaḥiah. C 9, executed together with C 8, defines the rights of Mivṭaḥiah's husband, Jezaniah b. Uriah, in the property. C 13 is a deed of conveyance of a house, by Maḥseiah to Mivṭaḥiah. C 14 is executed on the occasion of Mivṭaḥiah's divorce from her second husband, Pi' b. Paḥi: he renounces all claim to various chattels, on Mivṭaḥiah's swearing that they belong to her. C 15 is the deed of Mivṭaḥiah's third marriage, with Ashor b. Zeḥo.[1] C 20 and 25 are concerned with the settlement of claims made upon the sons of Mivṭaḥiah, Yedoniah and Maḥseiah. In C 28 the sons of Mivṭaḥiah divide between themselves slaves left by their mother. There is reason to assume that the archive as a whole passed into the hands of Mivṭaḥiah's son Yedoniah.[2]

The archive of Anani b. Azariah contains eleven documents, covering a period of forty-nine years (451–402 B.C.). It reflects the legal activities of Anani b. Azariah and of the members of his family: his wife Tamut, his daughter Yehoyishma, and his son-in-law, Yehoyishma's husband Anani b. Ḥaggai. K 1 concerns the acquisition of some object of unknown nature by Anani b. Azariah from one Mikha.[3] K 2 is the marriage document of Anani b. Azariah and the slave-girl Tamut. K 3 is a deed of sale: a house is sold to Anani b. Azariah by one Bagazusht and his wife Ubil. K 4 is a deed of gift. Anani b. Azariah gives to his wife Tamut half the house he has acquired in K 3. K 5 is a deed of manumission: *Tpmt* (= Anani's wife Tamut) and her daughter are manumitted. K 6 is a deed of gift. Anani b. Azariah gives a house to his daughter Yehoyishma. K 7 is the marriage document of Yehoyishma and Anani b. Ḥaggai. K 9 and 10 are

---

[1] In C 25 and 28 Ashor is called by the Jewish name Nathan; this indicates his becoming a Jew.

[2] See p. 67, below; C 48, a fragment of a betrothal agreement, conceivably also belongs to the archive. See Kraeling, p. 52.

[3] See RIDA v (1958), p. 299.

further deeds of gift by Anani b. Azariah to his daughter Yehoyishma. K 11 is a deed of loan: Anani b. Ḥaggai borrows a
quantity of spelt from Paḥnum b. *Bs'*. K 12 is a deed of sale.
Anani b. Azariah and his wife sell their house to their son-in-law,
Yehoyishma's husband Anani b. Ḥaggai.[1]

[1] The dominant view, that these eleven documents constitute a coherent archive,
has been challenged by E. Volterra, in his review of Kraeling, published in *Iura*,
vi (1955), pp. 349–60, and also in his 'Affrancazioni'. For a detailed examination
of his views see 'Identities'.

II

The Schema of the Documents

FROM the point of view of their schema the documents may be tentatively divided into two groups, an earlier one (Group A) and a later one (Group B).[1] The differences are not fundamental; on the contrary, they concern matters of minor importance, and only their accumulation suggests a distinction. Moreover, our material for group A is so scanty (and so poorly preserved) as to rule out definite statements. The division of the documents into two groups is here offered only as a working hypothesis, which only the discovery of additional material could substantiate—or disprove.

Group A comprises P. Meissner, C 1, 2, 3, 11, 46. P. Meissner has peculiarities of its own, possibly a consequence of its different place of provenance. The date is damaged in C 3 and missing in C 11 and 46, but I include them in this group since they show the features characteristic of it. No date can be suggested for C 46. As for C 11, Cowley submits that it was written about 455 B.C., but I should tentatively put it at 479 B.C.[2]

Group B comprises all the other documents. The earliest one belonging to it is C 5, of 471 B.C.

We can now discuss the various parts of the schema.

I. Date

The date forms the beginning of all the legal papyri.[3] Letters are, if at all, dated at the end (C 30, 31, 42, K 13).

Group A has Egyptian dating only, in the order: day, month, regnal year. E.g. C 1: 'On the 2nd day of the month of Epiphi,

---

[1] For a more detailed discussion see 'Schema'. [2] Cf. 'Schema', pp. 42 f.
[3] With the exception of C 44, a declaration on oath, which is not dated.

year 27 of Darius the king.' P. Meissner has a different order: regnal year, month, day: 'In the year 7 of the king Darius, month Meḥir, 6.'

Group B usually has double dating, Babylonian[1] and Egyptian. The Babylonian date is usually given first, but K 1 and 6, and possibly C 45, have the inverted order. Several papyri of group B have only Egyptian dates: C 7, 29, 35, K 11, 12. The same is probably the case in C 43, where there is no space for the Babylonian date inserted by Cowley. We do not know when C 43 was written, but C 29, 35, K 11, and 12 are all of the last decade of the fifth century.[2] Consequently the fact that they have only Egyptian dating is not connected with the similar usage in group A, the latest specimen of which is about seventy years earlier.

Kraeling (p. 51) regards the Babylonian dating as obligatory, but his opinion requires some qualification. It does not apply to the period of group A, and any obligation to use Babylonian dating had clearly fallen into desuetude by the end of the fifth century. The demotic papyri of the Persian era all have only Egyptian dating, but they are all contemporary with group A. Demotic documents corresponding in time to group B have not been discovered.

Several of the later documents, C 20, 29, K 7, 11, mention only the year and month, but not the day. It has been suggested that in such cases the first day of the month is meant,[3] but it seems preferable to assume assimilation to the Egyptian way of dating: the demotic documents of the Persian era are dated by year and month only.

II. *Place of Execution of the Document*

The date may be followed by a reference to the place where the document was executed: '. . . in Yeb (= Elephantine)', or

---

[1] Scholars disagree whether the dating is according to the Babylonian spring-to-spring calendar, or according to a Jewish autumn-to-autumn one. See S. H. Horn and L. H. Wood, JNES xiii (1954), pp. 1 ff.; R. Parker, ibid. xiv (1955), pp. 271 ff.

[2] C 7 is of the fourth year of Artaxerxes, that is either 461 (if the king is Artaxerxes I) or 401 (if the reference is to Artaxerxes II). That the dating is Egyptian only seems to be an argument in favour of the later date.   [3] Kraeling, p. 208.

'. . . in Syene'. But there are variations to be observed. Some papyri have this reference twice: once at the point just mentioned, a second time following the name of the scribe ('There wrote E son of F this document at Yeb'). In other cases the place of execution is given only in one of these two places, either after the date or after the name of the scribe. Other documents again omit any reference to the place of execution.

It follows that the omission of a reference to the place of execution can be asserted only in documents of which the beginning and the end is preserved. It is for this reason that it is difficult to come to a clear conclusion about group A. On the whole it seems that in this group it was not the practice to mention the place of execution.[1]

In group B a majority of the papyri do refer to the place of execution. However, there are eight complete documents which do not,[2] and it is therefore probable that even in the time of group B such a reference was not considered essential.

III. *Parties*

Group A: . . . said A son of B to C son of D as follows:

Group B: . . . said A son of B (description) to C son of D (description) as follows:

As can be readily seen, the difference is that, as a rule, in group A the names of the parties are not followed by any further description, whereas a description is usually added in group B: the parties are described by their place of residence, sometimes also by the military unit to which they belong or by their occupation. For example, in C 8: 1 f.: 'Maḥseiah b. Yedoniah, a Jew holding property in Yeb the fortress'; in C 14: 1 f.: 'Pi' b. Paḥi, builder, of Syene the fortress'; in K 2: 2 f.: 'Meshullam, b. Zakkur, Aramaean of Syene, of the *degel* of Warizath.[3]

Occasionally, the same person may be described one way in one document, another way in another. For example, Maḥseiah b. Yedoniah is an Aramaean of Syene, of the *degel* of Warizath (C 5), a Jew of Yeb the fortress, of the *degel* of Warizath (C 6),

---

[1] See 'Schema', p. 36. [2] C 5, 10, 13, 15, K 1, 2, 3, 4.

[3] For further details see 'Schema', p. 37.

a Jew of Yeb the fortress, of the *degel* of Haumdath (C 8, 9), and finally again an Aramaean of Syene, of the *degel* of Warizath (C 13, 15). The descriptions 'Jew' and 'Aramaean' interchange freely, the choice being determined mostly by the place of residence mentioned: Jews are usually from Yeb, Aramaeans from Syene. Differences relating to the *degel* show that a person could be transferred from one unit to another. When we are in a position to establish the identity of a person on other grounds, divergences of description may be safely discounted.[1]

IV. *Operative Part*

There is no difference between the two groups as far as the operative part of the document is concerned. It is invariably in subjective style. Usually one party only (A son of B) speaks, namely the party undertaking obligations. In most cases the obligation is unilateral since the other party has already fulfilled his part in the transaction: the lender has already given the money, the borrower now lists his duties; the buyer has paid the purchase price, the seller now undertakes not to interfere with him and to defend him against interference by others. There is no answer, no expression of assent by the other party to the transaction.

The closest approach to offer and acceptance occurs in the marriage contracts. There the bridegroom asserts as follows: 'I have come to thy house and asked of thee the woman Yehoyishma by name, thy sister, in wifehood. And thou didst give her to me.'[2] But even here, we should note, the person assenting is silent, nor is the acceptance couched in objective terms—it is still the bridegroom, whose request has been granted, who speaks. C 28, concerning the division of Mivṭaḥiah's inheritance, mentions that her sons have come to an agreement (*'ištawwena*) as to the share each one is to get.

Sometimes, in executory contracts, it is only to be expected that both parties should speak; the only alternative would be the writing of two documents, each setting out the obligations

---

[1] See Volterra, 'Affrancazioni', p. 690, note 2, and against his views 'Identities', pp. 353 f.   [2] K 7: 3 f.; and see 'Marriage Contracts', pp. 3 f.

of one party only, but things are usually not carried to that extreme.[1] Both parties speak, for example, in K 5, a deed of manumission. The document begins with the declaration of the manumitter that no one shall be able to enslave again the two slave-women who have been freed; they in turn bind themselves to render certain services to the manumitter and, on his decease, to his son. But even where, as in this case, both parties speak, there is no direct relationship of offer and acceptance, question and answer.

Certain clauses, it is true, are in certain contexts always couched in objective style. In the marriage contracts, references to death and divorce are objective; not '(if) I should die', but '(if) Anani should die'; not '(if) I should stand up in the congregation . . .', but '(if) Anani should stand up, &c.'.[2] This may be due to the fact that the bride is, formally, not a party to the contract.[3] Hence, in referring to actions of hers, objective formulation cannot be avoided; the husband's acts would in due course be described in a similar manner, and this usage might occasionally influence also other types of contracts.[4] But this is not the rule; in other contexts we find people speaking subjectively of their death.[5]

V. *Name of Scribe*

There wrote E son of F this document. . . .

The Elephantine documents invariably state the name of the scribe by whom they were written.[6] C 1 might appear to be an exception, but in reality it is not: it is merely that at the end of the document two lines are missing, the one containing the name of a witness, the other the name of a scribe. This is practically certain from a comparison with C 11.[7]

---

[1] See, however, K 8: 4, where reference is made to a document executed by the other party.

[2] See K 2: 7 ff., 7: 21 ff., C 15: 17 ff. Cf. pp. 54, 72, below.

[3] See p. 45, below.   [4] See C 5: 8.

[5] C 8: 3, 8; K 9: 17, 18; 10: 11, 13.

[6] C 44, the declaration on oath already mentioned, does not state the name of the writer; but this document is altogether different in its nature from all the others, and may be disregarded.   [7] 'Schema', pp. 38 f.

In four of the documents belonging to group A (P. Meissner, C 1, 11, 46) the list of witnesses precedes the name of the scribe. Seidl[1] points out that this sequence accords with Babylonian practice, but not with Egyptian.[2] The placing of the scribe at the end has the advantage that it will immediately be obvious if the document is not complete.

The sequence, witnesses-scribe or scribe-witnesses, may reflect the practice of merely listing the names of the witnesses, or of having them sign with their own hand. If the names are only listed, as is always the case in cuneiform documents, it is plausible for the scribe to complete his work by writing his name. Where, on the other hand, the witnesses sign *propria manu*, as is often the case in the demotic and Aramaic documents, the scribe finishes by writing his name, and it is only then that the signatures of the witnesses follow.

The scribes who drew up documents in Elephantine need not have been professionals, though some of them probably were. The outstanding scribes of the papyri are three: Nathan b. Anani, who wrote C 10, 13, 15, K 2, and perhaps C 45; his son Ma'uziah b. Nathan b. Anani, who wrote C 18, 20, 25, K 4, and 7; Ḥaggai b. Shemaiah, who wrote K 3, 9, 10, and 12. C 8 and 9, related in their contents, were written by the same person on the same day. All the other documents were written by different persons. Altogether the Elephantine papyri furnish us with the names of fifteen persons who drew up documents there in the course of the fifth century. The great number of persons functioning as scribes suggests that there was no need for special authorization. Apparently anyone was entitled to draw up documents. Nor did the law require the employment of someone not connected with the transaction: some of the documents were drawn up by one of the parties.[3]

The nationality of the scribes is of obvious importance, since it was their task to supply the proper formulas for the documents, to find the proper legal expression for the wishes of the

---

[1] *Rechtsgeschichte*, p. 17, note 23.
[2] In this point C 2 and 3 are in agreement with the documents of group B.
[3] 'Schema', pp. 41 f.

parties. In doing so a scribe would naturally draw on his own legal system, with which he was familiar. Foreign names might indicate *prima facie* that six of the fifteen persons who wrote the Elephantine papyri were non-Jews.[1] How far this criterion is reliable depends on the difficult question as to the significance of names. It is fairly certain that the bearer of a typically Jewish name was a Jew, but can the contrary be confidently maintained with regard to non-Jewish names? The material at our disposal permits of no conclusive answer, but instances in the Elephantine papyri in which a person definitely identifiable as Jewish bears a non-Jewish name are very rare.[2] At any rate the non-Jewish origin of at least some of the scribes seems probable enough.[3] If that is so, then it is of some importance that there appear to be no differences, formal or substantive, between the documents, which could be traced back to the different nationality of the scribes.

The documents vary considerably in the degree of care devoted to their execution. A few are free of errors or corrections, others have relatively many. The usual mistakes are cases of dittography (in these papyri always of the same kind, the doubling of a word) and of haplography (of various kinds: omission of a letter or, more frequently, of a word or words).

A peculiar mistake occurred in K 12, the document in which Anani b. Azariah and his wife sell their house to their son-in-law, the husband of Yehoyishma. In the first nine lines the scribe wrote down the introductory clauses usual in conveyances,[4] and started upon the description of the property transferred. The beginning of line 10 is rubbed out. He then started writing the document anew on a different papyrus. However, in the end he did not destroy the unfinished document: it was pasted on to the new, complete version, and the two have reached us together.

It is fairly certain what caused the re-writing: at the end of line 9, in the description of the boundaries, the house to the east is defined as 'the house which I gave to thee', i.e. to the buyer. Actually Anani b. Azariah had given the house to his daughter, the wife of the buyer. And indeed, the revised version is more carefully formulated: 'east of it is thy house . . . which we gave to Yehoyishma, our daughter.' We do not know what induced the scribe or the parties to preserve

---

[1] The persons who wrote C 8 (and 9), 14, 28, K 1, 8, 11.

[2] Cf. S. E. Loewenstamm, *Encyclopaedia Biblica*, iii, 1958, column 444 (Hebrew).

[3] See *Gifts*, p. 12.   [4] See p. 79, below.

the rejected first version. Perhaps it was that there are in it some details which are not mentioned in the revise: the name of the previous owners of the property, and the statement that the price has been paid in full.[1]

Many of the documents contain additions made by the scribe on re-reading: letters and words omitted in the haste of writing are inserted. Once, in K 3, the scribe, in his hurry, had forgotten the dictation clause.[2] Not all additions, however, are corrections in the strict sense. Sometimes insertions are made for the sake of clearness or completeness. So, for example, in C 5, the entire line 5 is an explanatory insertion. The additions *uverah* ('and daughter'), above line 5 of K 5, *zekhar* **weniqvah* ('male and female'), above K 3: 21, are designed to answer the question of interpretation to be encountered in many systems, whether the masculine ('son') includes the feminine ('daughter').[3]

Sometimes alterations in a document reflect last-minute changes in the agreement of the parties. The main instance is K 2, where apparently such changes were made in the dispositions in contemplation of the death of the husband and the wife. This was achieved by erasures in lines 11 and 12.[4] It is possible that the penal provision, inserted over line 14, was also decided upon at the last moment, upon the demand of the bridegroom, Anani b. Azariah.

The genuineness of additions and erasures is not attested either in the manner nowadays usual, by putting initials on the margin of the document, or—what is more relevant—in the manner provided for in the Talmudic sources.[5] It seems then that the main safeguard against forgeries lay in the fact that the document was folded and sealed, so that it would be difficult to open without leaving tell-tale traces.

---

[1] For further comments on the two beginnings of K 12, see Kraeling, p. 268, Ginsberg, p. 161, Rabinowitz, p. 132; cf. also my note in RIDA v (1958), pp. 308 f.

[2] See p. 15, below.

[3] See, concerning the meaning of Accadian *mārū*, Driver and Miles, p. 338; with regard to Hebrew *ben* and Latin *filius*, see *Gifts*, pp. 228 ff.

[4] See p. 70, below.

[5] See Tosefta Baba Bathra 11. 10; Palestinian Talmud Giṭṭin 50*c*; Babylonian Talmud Baba Bathra 161*b*.

VI. *Dictation Clause*

With a single exception (K 2), all the documents of group B are said to be written *kefum*—'at the dictation of' (literally 'according to the mouth of') the party speaking in the document. In K 2 there is no dictation clause.

Some of the documents were dictated by more than one person. There were two ways in which this might happen: two persons might act jointly, as when two plaintiffs execute a deed of 'removal' (or submission) (C 20); two brothers divide the inheritance of their mother (C 28); co-owners join in selling their property (K 3, 12). In these cases, to stress consent, expressions like *kol 2*—'all two',[1] or *kol 2 kefum ḥad*—'all two as by one mouth',[2] are used.

The other possibility is that both the parties to the document undertake obligations under it. So, for example, the marriage contract K 7 was dictated by the bridegroom Anani b. Ḥaggai, and by Zakkur b. Meshullam, who, having provided the dowry, now undertakes not to demand it back.[3]

So much for group B. As for group A, we are very much in the dark as to the clause under review. It is destroyed in C 1 and 46. P. Meissner, C 2 and 11 have the expression '*al pum* (or '*alpum*), instead of *kefum*. C 3 has **bikheḟi*. The meaning of neither of these expressions is quite clear. Of the four documents three, C 2, 3, 11, reflect special circumstances.[4] With regard to P. Meissner, in addition to the uncertainty of meaning, there is also the fact that it comes from a different place, hence may not serve as a basis for general conclusions. However, in the absence of sufficient grounds for differentiation, I shall tentatively attribute to the dictation clause in group A the same meaning it has in group B.

[1] C 20: 16; the expression occurs outside the dictation clause in C 28: 2, K 3: 10, 12: 3.
[2] K 12: 33 (see also line 11); similar expressions denoting unanimity occur in demotic documents, e.g. in P. Louvre 3228*d*, of 688 B.C., P. Turin 246, of 634 B.C. Cf. also Joshua 9. 2, 1 Kings 22. 13, 2 Chronicles 18. 12. Finally, see also Seneca, *Epistulae Morales*, 81. 31: *uno, quod aiunt, ore*.
[3] See also C 18: 4, and 'Schema', p. 40.
[4] For a detailed discussion, see 'Schema', pp. 41 ff.

VII. *Witnesses*

In group A the list of witnesses is preceded by the word *śahadayya'*—'the witnesses'. P. Meissner has *'eleh śahadayya'*—'these (are) the witnesses'.

In group B the list of witnesses is usually preceded by the words *śahadayya bego*—'the witnesses within' (or *weśahadayya' bego*—'and the witnesses within'); the phrase is omitted in three documents, C 6, 20, K 12.

Cowley does not attach any technical meaning to *bego*, and translates freely 'witnesses thereto'. He is followed by Kraeling, who, however, remarks (p. 137): 'The term could at times be taken more precisely, as the Mishnaic passage Baba Bathra 10. 1 clearly shows: *geṭ pašuṭ 'edaw mittokho umequššar 'edaw me'aḥoraw*—"a plain document has its witnesses within (on the recto); a tied up document has its witnesses on its back (the verso)".'[1]

Another argument in favour of the technical interpretation of *bego* is that most of the Aramaic documents in fact have the witnesses listed within,[2] whereas most of the contemporary demotic papyri are attested on the verso. The prevalent custom, therefore, was that the witnesses should sign, or be listed, on the back. That the Jews at Elephantine persisted in giving the witnesses within the document, contrary to the Egyptian practice of their day, shows that this was a peculiarity of their formular style to which they were long accustomed.[3] The express reference to this method of attestation (*bego*) may have been intended

---

[1] See already M. L. Margolis, *Jewish Quarterly Review*, N.S. ii (1912), p. 438, note 64. The suggestion that *śahadayya' bego* has a technical meaning is supported also by a Judaean deed of sale, of A.D. 134. Line 16 reads: *ke[tha]vah denah pešiṭ waḥathamu begawweh*—'this document is simple and they signed within'. See the translation and comment of J. T. Milik, *Revue Biblique*, lxi (1954), pp. 182 ff., and the comments of J. J. Rabinowitz, *Bulletin of the American Schools of Oriental Research*, cxxxvi (1954), p. 16.

[2] Exceptions: P. Meissner and C 2 are attested on the verso, probably because of lack of space; C 3 (duplicate of C 2?) has the witnesses on the recto. C 8 seems, according to the plate, to have seven witnesses within and five on the verso (there is no remark of Cowley on this). C 9 is written on both sides of the papyrus.

[3] But in Jeremiah 32. 10 the deed is attested on the verso. For detailed remarks on *śahadayya' bego*, see also Rabinowitz, pp. 155 ff.

to stress that the deviation from Egyptian usage was on purpose, and did not affect the validity of the document.

In one papyrus, C 13, a conveyance, the list of witnesses is preceded by the signature of the transferor, who signs *bekhi nafšeh*—'for himself'. That the signature of a party to the contract was devoid of legal effect is shown by the fact that this is the only Elephantine papyrus in which it occurs. It was the signature of the witnesses that was of legal import, not that of the parties; the latter seems here to be added for the sake of emphasis, without any further implication. In the demotic papyri too, though it is unusual for a party to sign the contract, it does occasionally happen.[1] The documents from Wadi Murabba'at (first and second centuries A.D.) are, as a rule, signed by the executing party, '*al nafšeh*—'for himself'.[2]

The witnesses sometimes sign themselves, sometimes their names are listed by the scribe. Even though at Elephantine literacy seems to have been quite common, a rule requiring that a witness should sign himself might have deprived part of the population of the capacity to act as witnesses, and obviously did not exist.

As a rule the patronymics of the witnesses are given, but exceptions occur; see K 4: 24, 11: 13, 12: 34. P. Meissner, however, is very unusual in omitting the patronymics of all the witnesses.

We now come to the vexed question of the number of witnesses. There is in this respect no difference between the two groups. Altogether there are twenty-nine documents in which either the final part of the papyrus enumerating the witnesses is complete, or at least the number of witnesses can be ascertained with a fair degree of probability.

Of these twenty-nine documents:

    one has three witnesses (K 2);
    fourteen have four witnesses (C 1,[3] 10, 11, 14, 15, 18, 20, 28, 43,[4] K 3, 4, 5, 11, 12);

---

[1] See E. Seidl, *Demotische Urkundenlehre*, 1937, p. 6, note 5.
[2] See, for example, P. Murabba'at 18, 19, 24, 42; also the Judaean deed of sale mentioned above (p. 16, note 1).
[3] See 'Schema', p. 47.   [4] Ibid., pp. 47 f.

one has five witnesses (C 13);

one has six witnesses (K 7);

eight have eight witnesses (C 2,[1] 5, 6, 25, 46, K 8, 9, 10);

two have nine (?) witnesses (P. Meissner,[2] K 1[3]);

two have twelve witnesses (C 8, 9).

If, for the moment, we leave aside K 2 and 7, the marriage contracts of Tamut and of her daughter Yehoyishma, the pattern seems plain: the key numbers are four and eight.[4] We have fifteen transactions which apparently require at least four witnesses, and twelve transactions apparently requiring at least eight witnesses. We shall later justify the inclusion of C 13 in the former group, of P. Meissner, K 1, C 8 and 9 in the latter.[5]

In an attempt to discover the criterion, if any, underlying the division into 'four witnesses documents' and 'eight witnesses documents', I have tried to broaden the basis of the inquiry by extending it to the contemporary demotic material.[6] This can be justified by the fact that the Aramaic papyri do not reveal any trace of an autonomous Jewish jurisdiction. It is therefore probable that disputes arising out of Aramaic contracts and disputes arising out of demotic contracts were brought before the same forum, and that they would have to answer the same requirements as to the number of witnesses.[7]

The matter has been investigated by Seidl,[8] who does not think a precise solution possible: 'Die Zahl der Zeugen schwankt; man kann aber ungefähr sagen: je wichtiger das Objekt ist, umso größer ist die Zahl der Zeugen.' Seidl goes on to give full details of the demotic documents, having from 1 to 21 witnesses. Perhaps it is possible to attain greater precision by paying attention also to the data of the Aramaic papyri, and above all by bearing in mind the possibility of development and change. *Non constat* that the Saitic and Persian periods form one definite entity.

On the whole, in the Saitic period the number of witnesses in

---

[1] See 'Schema', p. 47.   [2] Ibid., pp. 46 f.

[3] Ibid., p. 48.   [4] See already Pritsch, p. 17.

[5] See p. 20, below.   [6] See 'Schema', pp. 48 f.

[7] We are not, at the moment, concerned with a general comparison of the Aramaic and the demotic documents.   [8] *Rechtsgeschichte*, pp. 21 ff.

the demotic papyri is large,[1] and irregular. For example, eight papyri of the 'normal' style,[2] of the reign of Amasis II, listed by Griffith, have the following number of witnesses: 11, 13, 15, 16 [2], 19, 21, and 28.

But a short time before the Persian conquest, the demotic papyri evince the pattern suggested, as we saw, by the Aramaic papyri. Three documents of the year 525 each have four witnesses.[3] With very few exceptions[4] this pattern of four and eight witnesses is observed throughout the period here relevant.[5] Altogether we have to deal with twenty-two demotic papyri of this kind, following Seidl's lists with some minor additions. Of these 22 documents, 13 have four witnesses, 9 have eight.

Let us now classify the documents, demotic and Aramaic, having four witnesses:[6]

Sale (Moveables and Immoveables): C 13,[7] K 3, 12, P. Loeb 43 [73],[8] 44 [114a], 68 [95], P. Turin . . . [93],[9] P. Louvre 9292 [102].

Barter: C 1, 43, P. Turin . . . (F) [116].[10]

Division of Property: C 28.

Loan: C 10, 11, K 11, P. Strassburg 4 [118].

---

[1] But the only documents having less than four witnesses are just of this period; they are P. Louvre 7836 (535 B.C.), having two witnesses, and P. Louvre 7839 (533 B.C.), having one witness only.

[2] For a discussion of the 'normal' and the 'abnormal' style of Egyptian documents, see F. Ll. Griffith, *Catalogue of the Demotic Papyri in the John Rylands Library*, vol. iii (1909), pp. 12 ff.

[3] P. Strassburg 2 (conveyance of geese), P. Loeb 41 (establishing joint ownership over a cow), and P. Loeb 43 (conveyance of an ass).

[4] The only exceptions listed by Seidl are P. Cairo Spiegelberg 50059 (521 B.C.), a transfer of priestly income—21 witnesses; P. British Museum 10120 A and B (517 B.C.), a marriage settlement and division of property—9 witnesses; P. Louvre 3231a (497 B.C.), a gift of land—7 witnesses (is the document complete?).

[5] It has already been pointed out above (p. 8) that so far no demotic documents of the fifth century B.C. after the reign of Darius I have been forthcoming; documents later than 400 B.C. may here be disregarded.

[6] Including C 13, which has 5 witnesses.

[7] But see p. 3, note 4, above.

[8] The number in square brackets is that which the document is given in Seidl's list, at the end of his *Rechtsgeschichte*.

[9] This papyrus is not considered by Seidl in his discussion of witnesses; the same is true of P. Turin . . . (F), P. Turin 231, P. Bibliothèque Nationale 216, 217, P. Louvre 9293. In these instances the data of Griffith's *Catalogue* (see note 2, above) are followed.   [10] See the preceding footnote.

'Removal' from Claim (to moveables): C 14, 20.
Partnership: P. Strassburg 2 [75], P. Loeb 41 [74], 47 [111].
Marriage Contracts: C 15, 18, P. Berlin 3078 [103].
Divorce: P. Berlin 3076 [89], 3077 [113].
Manumission: K 5.
Gift of House: K 4.

A classification of the documents having eight witnesses[1]
gives the following result:

Gift of House (or Land): C 8, 46, K 9, 10, P. Turin 231 [90].[2]
Lease: P. Meissner, P. Loeb 45 [98].
'Removal' (or Conveyance) following Litigation: C 6, 25, K 1.[3]
Contract relating to the Reversion of Property: C 9.
Contract relating to Building Rights: C 5.
Endowment of Child: P. Bibliothèque Nationale 216 [84],[2]
      217 [85].[2]
Adoption: K 8.
Sale of Right to Inheritance: P. Louvre 9204 [106].
Guarantee (of return of a cow given to be spayed): P. Ber-
      lin 3110 [115].
Loan: P. Louvre 9293 [96].[2]
Sale (of House-site): P. Louvre 7128 [91].
Divorce: P. Berlin 3079 [110].

The number of witnesses attesting a document does not
necessarily coincide with the number required by law. The law
would lay down only a minimum number, but no harm would
be done if a document was signed by more. *Superflua non nocent.*

It is for this reason that I have included C 13, a deed of sale having
five witnesses, among the 'four witnesses documents', and P. Meissner
and K 1, each of which has perhaps nine witnesses, among the 'eight
witnesses documents'. I have also included in this group C 8 and 9,
with twelve witnesses each. C 8 is a deed of gift of a building plot,
and falls easily into line with the other deeds of gift listed. As for C 9,
we have no document exactly similar, but if one bears in mind the
picture as a whole, here too probably eight witnesses only were

---

[1] Including C 8 and 9, which have twelve witnesses, P. Meissner and K 1, which
perhaps have nine.
[2] See p. 19, note 9, above.   [3] Cf. RIDA v (1958), pp. 299 ff.

required. The great number of witnesses in these two documents may perhaps be due to the fact that three of them are closely related to the parties. We shall return to this point.

There are further complicating factors, which make it difficult to obtain reliable results. *Abundans cautela* may cause over-attestation. A comparison of the two lists suggests that several of the demotic documents attested by eight witnesses would have needed only four: the deed of loan P. Louvre 9293; the deed of sale P. Louvre 7128; and the deed of divorce P. Berlin 3079.

On the other hand, it is possible that now and then, because of ignorance or negligence, the number of witnesses may fall short of the legal requirements. This may have happened in K 4: it seems that the document, which has four witnesses, really required eight. This is the deed wherein Anani b. Azariah donates half a house to his wife Tamut. Since five other deeds of gift all have eight witnesses, we must come to the reluctant conclusion that K 4 was not sufficiently attested. In case of a dispute this might have caused trouble to the donee. As a matter of fact, we know that nothing of the sort happened: in K 12, some thirty-two years later, Anani and his wife join in selling the house to their son-in-law.

In other respects too our results are bound to be tentative. For example, we cannot know whether the distinction between 'removal' from claims to moveables and 'removal' from claims to land is a real one, or whether the documents of the latter kind, having eight witnesses, are over-attested.

Taking into account the various rectifications, the following scheme emerges:

Four witnesses	Eight witnesses
Sale of Land	Gift of Land
Barter	Lease
Division of Property	Sale of Right to Inheritance
Loan	Building Rights
'Removal' from Claim (to moveables)	'Removal' from Claim (to land), or Conveyances following Litigation
Partnership	
Marriage Contracts	Guarantee of Return of Cow
Divorce	Endowment of Child
Manumission	Adoption

The most interesting fact in this scheme is the distinction between sale and gift. It shows that, in general at least, the distinction between 'four witnesses documents' and 'eight witnesses documents' was not based upon the distinction between moveables and land, nor did it depend upon the value of the object. It will be clear now why I hesitate to treat the abandonment of claims ('removal') as an exception.

It is hardly likely that the division into 'four witnesses documents' and 'eight witnesses documents' is the result of some slow historical growth. What must have happened is that where previously there had been much arbitrariness, a deliberate reform, by way of enactment, introduced a definite system. The exact nature of this system is not too clear; tentatively one might suggest that the enactment gave a list of the more usual contracts of everyday life. These had already become stereotyped and were considered to be sufficiently attested if they bore the names of four witnesses. For all other documents not included in that list, eight witnesses were required. Our lists show that on the whole the documents having eight witnesses were of a more complicated legal character; but deeds of lease would be an exception. Gifts are a category apart, because of the lack of consideration.

We must now consider K 2 and 7, the marriage contracts of Tamut and of her daughter Yehoyishma, respectively.

K 2 has only three witnesses. This cannot be due to a slip. A document might by mistake be signed by four instead of eight witnesses, or *vice versa*. Tamut's marriage contract was drawn up by Nathan b. Azariah, apparently a professional scribe, at a time when the system of four and eight witnesses had already been in force for some three generations. The contracting parties, the bridegroom and Tamut's master, had previously been parties to transactions fully attested (see C 10, K 1). Special rules for the attestation of marriage contracts are not likely to have existed: other marriage contracts, C 15, 18, P. Berlin 3078, evidence the number of four witnesses for this type of document.

With all reserve one might suggest that the smaller number of witnesses may perhaps be due to the status of the bride, Tamut. It may have been customary to have fewer witnesses in writing a marriage contract of a slave-girl.

Though in the absence of further material it is impossible to prove a suggestion of this kind, it may derive a measure of support from the marriage contract of Tamut's daughter. Here too the number of witnesses, six, is quite unusual. It may reflect a desire to disguise her lowly status as a freedwoman. However, all she can get is the double of three, but not the four witnesses usual in the marriage contract of a freeborn bride.

A few minor points remain to be discussed:

The designation *śahed*—'witness' often appears before the name of a witness. But there is little regularity. Sometimes the designation precedes the name of every witness in the document (see, for example, K 10); more often some are so designated, others are not. In other documents, again, no one is so designated individually; we find only the general introductory *śahadayya' bego*—'the witnesses within' (e.g. K 7).

At Elephantine, as usually in the ancient world, testimony was a man's business.[1] The Aramaic papyri reveal women as holders of property; they can litigate and may be called upon to take an oath (C 6, 14). But there are in these documents no female witnesses. Whether they were competent to testify in court, as distinct from attesting legal transactions, we do not know.

A party was probably not a competent witness *in re sua*. Hence his signature to the document would carry little weight, and occurs only exceptionally, in C 13, signed by the man on whose behalf it was written.

On the other hand, we do find relatives of the parties among the witnesses. In C 8, where Maḥseiah b. Yedoniah donates a building-plot to his daughter Mivṭaḥiah, two of the witnesses are sons of the donor and one is his grandson. The signatures of the members of the family were probably intended to preclude any possibility that they might at some later time contest the validity of the transaction.[2] Whether such signatories were regarded as fully qualified witnesses we cannot know. To be sure, in C 8 each is specifically described as 'witness', but, as the document bears twelve signatures, the exclusion of the three

---

[1] See, however, Seidl, *Einführung*, p. 43.

[2] Cf. M. Schorr, UAZP, p. xxxv: *Durch ihre Zeugenschaft sollen sie sich ihrer eventuellen Einspruchsrechte begeben und ihre Willenszustimmung zum Vertrag ausdrücken*; see also P. Koschaker, *Babylonisch-assyrisches Bürgschaftsrecht*, 1911, p. 205. For the corresponding Talmudic provisions see Mishnah Kethuboth 13. 6.

relatives would not invalidate it. We can imagine that a man might be estopped by his signature from attacking a contract, even though he would not be competent to testify in a conflict between the parties. The same witnesses appear also in C 9, a document executed on the same day as C 8, and containing further arrangements concerning the same property.

In C 25, an abandonment of claim ('removal'), one of the eight witnesses, Maḥseiah b. Yedoniah, is apparently a cousin of the defendants in whose favour the document is executed. He clearly has nothing to do with the transaction and signs as an ordinary witness.[1]

VIII. *Endorsement*

The two groups have much the same endorsement. It is written on the outside of the document, after this has been rolled up, tied, and sealed.[2] It is usually a short memorandum enabling the holder of several sealed rolls to know what each is about.[3]

Since the endorsement is on the outside of the document, it is natural that in many cases it has been lost. Still there remain quite a number; indeed, in one case, K 15, we have only the endorsement, while of the document itself nothing is left.

The endorsement usually contains the names of the parties to the transaction. As a rule it gives a general idea of the contents of the document, e.g. 'document of a house which A son of B wrote to C son of D.' Sometimes it is a little more elaborate (e.g. C 25, 28). On other occasions, again, it contains only the names of the parties, without any clue to the contents (C 2): 'The document which Hoshea and Aḥiav wrote to Espemeṭ' (see also C 13, K 15).[4]

---

[1] According to Cowley, in C 1 the witness Shelomem b. Azariah may have been the father of one of the parties, Yah'or *berath* Shelomem. The mere identity of the name, however, does not warrant this suggestion.　　　[2] See Cowley, p. 7.

[3] Kraeling, p. 150; for a picture of sealed and endorsed papyri see Kraeling, plate xxi.

[4] Somewhat exceptional is the endorsement of K 2: 'Tamut brought in to Anani in her hand silver, one karsh, five shekels.' It is not what one would expect as the summary of a marriage contract. Moreover, Tamut's master is not referred to, though he was party to the contract. (Also the sum mentioned is different from that given inside.) See p. 57, below, for further details.

L. Wenger thinks that these endorsements developed out of the *scriptura exterior* of 'double documents' (*Doppelurkunden*) and were originally much more detailed. In his opinion they are but *zusammengeschrumpfte Außenschriften*—reduced *scripturae exteriores*.[1] However, even if no *Doppelurkunde* had ever existed, whenever documents are sealed, some sort of inscription is obviously necessary, in order that the owner may be able to distinguish between his various scrolls.[2]

The schemata of the two groups, A and B, can now be set out:

Group A:

1. *Date*: On the *n*th day of the month (Egyptian month-name), year *x* of Y the king.
2. *Parties*: . . . said A son of B to C son of D as follows:
3. *Operative Part.*
4. *Witnesses*: The witnesses: J son of K, L son of M, &c.
5. *Name of Scribe*: There wrote E son of F this document . . .
6. *Dictation Clause* (?): . . . at the dictation of A son of B.
7. *Endorsement* (on the verso): A document of (name of transaction), which A son of B wrote to C son of D.

Group B:

1. *Date*: On the *m*th of (Babylonian month), that is the *n*th day of (Egyptian month), year *x* of Y the king,
2. *Place of Execution*: . . . in (name of place) . . .
3. *Parties*: . . . said A son of B (description) to C son of D (description) as follows:
4. *Operative Part.*
5. *Name of Scribe*: There wrote E son of F this document . . .
6. *Dictation Clause*: . . . at the dictation of A son of B.
7. *Witnesses*: The witnesses (are written) within: J son of K, L son of M, &c.
8. *Endorsement* (on the verso): A document of (name of transaction) which A son of B wrote to C son of D.

---

[1] *Zeitschrift der Savigny-Stiftung für Rechtsgeschichte, Romanistische Abteilung*, xlii (1922), p. 626; his view is accepted by H. Steinacker, *Die antike Grundlage der frühmittelalterlichen Urkunde*, 1927, p. 165, note 6.
[2] See already W. Kunkel, *Studi Riccobono*, i, 1936, p. 416, note 8.

I have already stressed that the differences between the two groups are not fundamental, and we cannot know why such slight changes as there are took place. Some of the innovations, for example the double dating, may be due to regulations laid down by the authorities. We should probably be able to be more definite if demotic papyri corresponding in time to the transition from group A to group B were available for comparison. As already mentioned, up to now no such documents have been published.

III

Courts and Procedure

WE know very little indeed about the courts having jurisdiction in disputes between inhabitants of Elephantine. It is noteworthy that the papyri reveal no trace of any autonomous Jewish tribunal.[1] All legal business apparently comes before the court of the state or the commander of the garrison. C 1 refers to a decision given jointly by the king's judges (*dayyane malka'*) and the commander of the garrison (*rav ḥayla'*). C 6 mentions a complaint lodged before Damidata 'and his colleagues the judges'; the name of the person presiding is Persian, and this is suggestive of the nature of the tribunal. The fragmentary and very obscure C 16 refers to litigation in which the commander of the garrison is one of the persons called upon to adjudicate. C 20 refers to a dispute concerning chattels alleged to have been deposited with a man who has meanwhile died. The case had been heard by the governor (**fratarak*)[2] and the commander of the garrison. C 25 is a deed of 'removal', probably following upon litigation; the deed is made before the commander of the garrison. K 8, also made before the commander, concerns adoption.

In several documents[3] mention is made of the addressees of possible future complaints. Some variations are to be observed: C 8 and 10 have *segan wedayyan*; C 47, K 9 and 10 have *segan umare'*; K 1 has *dayyan umare'*; finally, K 12 combines all three, *segan umare' wedayyan*. The distinctions between the various designations are not quite clear. *Dayyan* means 'judge', the other terms no doubt refer to other officials. *Segan*, usually translated 'governor', 'prefect', occurs most regularly; it is omitted only in K 1. At any rate the picture is similar to that which obtains in many ancient systems, namely there is little separation of

---

[1] See already p. 18, above.   [2] See Cowley, p. 59.
[3] C 8, 10, 47, K 1, 9, 10, 12.

powers, and a great part of the litigation may come before the functionaries entrusted with the administration of the country, the executive as we should call it.

The *'edah*, the community as a whole or some representative part of it, is mentioned as the forum before which declarations of divorce (*śin'ah*) may be made. We have no ground for attributing a judicial nature to the function of the *'edah*; it merely provides for the necessary publicity.[1] This would prevent subsequent uncertainty and possible allegations of adultery against the divorced wife.

About the actual steps to be taken to start a suit we are almost completely in the dark. Of the documents just mentioned most refer to litigation and tribunals only incidentally; their main purpose is to record the state of affairs existing after litigation, the end-result. Only C 7, 16, and 44 are documents of a purely preliminary, procedural nature: C 7, perhaps a summons on a charge of assault and theft; C 16, a complaint about some wrong suffered by the petitioner; C 44, a declaration on oath. Also C 49 may concern an action for the recovery of a debt. All these four are little more than obscure fragments; since they did not purport actually to determine rights, less care was devoted to their preservation than to that, for example, of deeds of sale and gift.

References to possible litigation are indeed abundant in the contracts. But they are of little help in finding out about points of procedure. The terms usually employed are *gari din (udevav)* or *rešah din (udevav)*—'to start suit (or process)', 'to litigate', or *qeval 'al X (qodam)* . . .—'to complain about X (before) . . .'. From these one can draw no conclusions, for example, concerning the question whether proceedings were predominantly oral or whether at least the initial stages were in writing; not to mention the fact that conclusions from terminology are generally precarious. A term, while it might reflect the actual procedure of the time of the documents, might equally well be a survival from some earlier stage. It is precisely in procedure that terminology tends to remain unchanged, even if no longer corresponding to reality.[2]

---

[1] But compare the biblical *'edah*, e.g. Numbers 35. 24.
[2] Cf. Seidl, *Rechtsgeschichte*, p. 38.

There are no Aramaic documents actually describing the proceedings before a court; neither are there judgements. As a consequence we know next to nothing about rules of evidence. Indeed none of our documents mentions anyone but the parties making a statement before a court in the course of litigation. But then we must recall that the material at our disposal on this point is very limited. Actually there are indications pointing the other way, in documents not at all concerned with litigation: conveyances, marriage contracts, deeds of loan, &c. We have seen[1] that all of them are signed by (or on behalf of) male witnesses. It stands to reason that these might eventually be called upon to testify; either to the genuineness of their signature, or also to the actual contents of the transaction: the main object of calling in witnesses must surely be to make certain that, if necessary, evidence will be available.

We do not know what degree of freedom a judge enjoyed in evaluating evidence. Our conclusions as to the number of witnesses required suggest that the judge would have to insist on a fixed minimum number. It seems also that the parties could make certain binding arrangements—binding on themselves and binding on the court—with regard to the evidentiary force of a document. In C 10, a deed of loan, the borrower declares: 'I shall not be able to say to thee that I have paid thee thy silver and its interest while this document is in thy hand.' In other words, the document in the hands of the lender is conclusive evidence of his not having been repaid. Witnesses to the contrary will be of no avail.[2] But a receipt given by the lender would probably be accepted as evidence; this would be useful, if for some reason a deed of loan could not be returned.[3] It is inevitable where, as in C 10 and 11, the monthly payment of interest was envisaged, and indeed C 11 provides for the writing of a receipt for each instalment.

Some conveyances declare that any further document purporting to come from the hands of the alienor is a forgery, not to

---

[1] pp. 16 ff., above.
[2] Similar provisions occur in demotic deeds of loan; cf. Seidl, *Rechtsgeschichte*, p. 36.
[3] See EL 191, 192; UAZP 238: receipts declaring deeds of loan to be void.

be accepted as evidence. So, with variations, C 8, 13, K 9, 10. For example, C 8: 15: 'And they shall not be able to produce against thee a document new or old in my name concerning that land, to give it to someone else. The document which they will produce against thee will be forged; not I have written it and it shall not be accepted in litigation while this document is in thy hand.' We should like to know what force a court would give to such a clause. The point really at issue can hardly have been forgery properly so called. Whether a document is forged or not must be decided not on the basis of what is said in the document itself (a forged document might declare all others forged), but by independent examination.[1] It may rather be tentatively suggested that the clause constitutes a device designed to avoid resort to the rules of substantive law, where these were inadequate and did not conform to the wishes of the parties. Three of the four documents containing the clause are deeds of gift, and we do not know exactly how far a gift bound the donor. It is quite possible that, in the absence of special arrangements, gifts were revocable because of the lack of consideration.[2] If so a second alienee might successfully attack the gift. The clause under discussion would prevent this; it would render the gift irrevocable. It is interesting that the clause uses procedural machinery to this end. It does not lay down in so many words that the gift should stand, but provides that the document cannot be contested.

There is a comparable provision in two marriage contracts, C 18, K 7. In both the person providing the dowry promises not to reclaim it; should he nevertheless do so, he 'shall not be listened to' (*la' yištema' leh*). Here too, it seems, an act which may be of doubtful finality in substantive law (namely the giving of a dowry) is reinforced on the procedural plane.

The phrase *wela' din udevav* (occasionally more briefly *wela' din*)—'and no suit or process (shall obtain)' is of doubtful import. It occurs quite frequently,[3] and, literally, it means that legal

---

[1] Cf. Seidl, ibid.

[2] Cf. ibid., pp. 40 ff., for the principle of *notwendige Entgeltlichkeit*.

[3] C 8: 14, 21; 9: 15; 14: 10; 15: 29; 20: 16; 25: 17; 28: 12, 14; K 4: 15, 22; 5: 15; 11: 8, 12.

steps which the person executing the document (or some third person) might contemplate shall be of no avail. However, just what effect the courts would give to the phrase there is no means of knowing.

We have seen that, apart from the isolated instance of C 13, parties do not add their signatures to the document, and I deduced from this that they are not competent witnesses *in sua causa*. But it would be wrong to assume further that the parties are silent in court. Several times we find disputes decided on the basis of statements made by a party, apparently (always?) under oath. C 6 tells of an oath by the defendant, his wife, and his son, in a litigation concerning the ownership of a piece of land. It seems probable that where no other evidence is available, a claimant, as an ultimate step, may request the court to impose an oath upon the defendant. Having nothing to lose, he relies on this oath of his opponent. In the fifth century B.C. an oath is a serious matter indeed, and a litigant would rarely dare to bring on himself the wrath of the deity by taking a false oath. Hence if the defendant does not shrink from swearing, that is decisive. The happenings of C 6 are referred to five years later, in C 8: 23–26. C 6 is being handed over to the donee, to serve as evidence, in case the unsuccessful claimant of C 6 should make a further attempt at litigation: 'There is also a document of removal (*sefar mirḥaq*) which Dargman b. Ḥarshin the Khorazmian wrote for me concerning that land, when he laid claim to it before the judges and an oath to him was imposed upon me and I swore to him that it was mine, and he wrote a document of removal and gave (it) to me. This document I have given to thee. Thou keep it. If tomorrow or another day Dargman or a son of his should lay claim to that plot, produce that document, and contest the case against him.'[1]

The fragmentary C 7 is tantalizing; its sense is difficult to make out. What is clear is that it refers to a charge of assault and theft, and to declarations to be made in this connexion by the defendant. The restorations of the document which have been

[1] In other cases old title-deeds are handed over to the alienee. See C 13: 6, K 12: 31.

attempted are far too problematic to warrant any conclusion.[1] Another delict seems to be the subject matter of C 45; an oath is imposed upon a party, apparently charged with stealing fish. This document also is too fragmentary to be intelligible.

C 14 is a deed executed by a husband: he declares himself well satisfied with the oath rendered at his request by his divorcee. The oath establishes conclusively the wife's rights with regard to a variety of chattels ('. . . silver and corn and garments and copper and iron, all goods and possessions, and the marriage document').

In all these cases the oath is mentioned only incidentally; it is not the main topic of the document. C 44 is different. If correctly restored, it is the text of an oath taken by the defendant in the course of the litigation (concerning the ownership of an ass).

All oaths are taken by the deity, that is usually by Yahu; a deity Anathyahu is mentioned in C 44.[2] Contrary to widespread Oriental and Egyptian practice, oaths by the sovereign do not occur, a peculiarity probably accounted for by religious scruples. Even this precaution would not avoid all religious difficulties: in C 14 Mivṭaḥiah, a Jewess, has to take an oath by the Egyptian goddess Sati. This is interesting, since modern reasoning would regard an oath as more satisfactory if taken by the deity of the person swearing: it is more likely to put 'the fear of god' into his bones. Yet apparently here the identity of the opponent, an Egyptian in this case, is the decisive factor.

All oaths in the Aramaic papyri are assertory, solemn declarations as to the existence of a fact or facts. There is no case of a promissory oath, whereby a party solemnizes an undertaking as to his future behaviour; to ensure that obligations will be honoured resort is usually had to penal stipulations.[3] As a rule the oaths are 'oaths of clearance' (*Reinigungseide*), designed to refute a charge and clear the defendant.[4] A situation *sui generis*,

---

[1] The wording of the document has parallels in Driver, Letter 12: 8 f.

[2] Cf. Kraeling, p. 91.

[3] See p. 86, below.

[4] In this they resemble the biblical oath; see, for example, Exodus 22. 10, and cf. also the oath mentioned in Leviticus 5. 22.

apparently reflecting a special rule of the law of divorce, obtains in C 14. It is likely that in this case the wife taking the oath is the claimant, demanding the return of her dowry; however, the document leaves the roles of plaintiff and defendant unattributed, speaking equivocally of 'the action which we took' (*dina' zi 'avadna*).[1] But apart from C 14 there is no instance of a case being decided in favour of a plaintiff on the strength of his oath.[2] In the main, the oath at Elephantine is a means of defence, not of attack.

Several times it is stated that a party has been interrogated (*še'il*). Occasionally this is a step preceding the taking of an oath; so apparently in C 7: 6, 45: 3 f.[3] We do not know whether the behaviour of the defendant when interrogated would in any way influence his capacity to take an oath. In other words, we do not know whether a court was entitled to deny the oath to a defendant who had not stood up well to being interrogated. If there was such a possibility then we may assume that the right to the decisive oath would pass to the plaintiff (but there is no such case in our material). Comparable rules, even though in different circumstances, are met in Talmudic law.[4]

When judgement is duly given, there still remains the question of its execution. The papyri convey no information on this matter. But we have seen that deeds of 'removal' or 'submission' executed by the party (plaintiff or defendant) renouncing a claim are fairly frequent. I am deliberately using the vague phrase, 'the party renouncing a claim': he may do so because he has lost his case, but also because he has received satisfaction, full or partial. The latter possibility is underlined by the fact that the notion of 'removal' occurs where the receipt of a consideration is expressly confirmed, as in C 13, K 3. But most of our documents of removal are instances of the former application.

So in C 6 the plaintiff, having lost his case, declares himself unable to lay further claims to the property.[5] In the endorsement the docu-

---

[1] For further discussion of C 14, see p. 63, below.
[2] For such cases see, for example, Mishnah Shevu'oth 7. 1, 2, 3, 5.
[3] But in C 16: 3, 20: 8, no mention is made of an oath. With regard to *še'il*, see also Driver, p. 17. [4] See Mishnah Shevu'oth 7. 1, 4.
[5] For the interpretation of this document see 'Conveyances', p. 249.

ment is called a *sefar mirḥaq*, a deed of 'removal'. Similarly in C 14, at the end of the litigation the husband declares that he has removed (*reḥaq*) from the wife with regard to the chattels in dispute. Concerning C 20 it has been suggested[1] that it is executed by the winners, who, on receiving satisfaction, renounce further claims. We have seen that such a construction is possible, yet there appears to be no support for it in the document. The decisive sentence is: '. . . then you were interrogated and you . . . have satisfied our heart concerning these goods, and we are satisfied therewith.' Hence, it is likely that this case, like the others, ended in the defeat of the plaintiffs. C 25 apparently concerns litigation in a matter of inheritance (though this is not said in so many words); here too the loser (apparently the plaintiff) declares his 'removal' from his adversaries and from the property.[2]

It is significant that the loser has to declare his submission, his acquiescence in the state of affairs decided upon by the court. The declaration of the party is endowed with greater effectiveness, it seems, than the actual decision of a judicial body. Not impossibly in certain cases a judgement properly so called is dispensed with altogether; the court may confine itself to directing the litigation and helping the parties to reach a final settlement in a semi-independent way, persuading them and exerting pressure where necessary. It is the submission of the loser which creates the true barrier against any attempt on his part to resume the litigation. The various stages of litigation come out clearly in C 8: 23 ff.: (*a*) the plaintiff brought his claim, (*b*) I swore, and (*c*) he wrote a deed of submission.[3] There is no mention of a decision by the court. Perhaps all the judges actually did was to order the writing of the deed of submission. One must, of course, not deduce that this is necessarily so in every case: C 1 speaks of property which 'the judges of the king gave' to the person executing the document.

On the whole, then, it is not unlikely that the execution of a decision—whether it is a proper decision or only advice with some threat of pressure, whether formal or informal—is closely associated with the declaration of submission issuing from the loser. Needless to say, where the plaintiff is the loser there is no

---

[1] Cowley, p. 57; Pritsch, p. 49.
[2] A more detailed discussion of this document is given at p. 75, below.
[3] See the quotation, p. 31, above.

room for any execution, and the deed of submission is aimed only at preventing further litigation on the same matter.[1]

From execution one must distinguish the taking of pledges, provided for in the deeds of loan C 10 and K 11. The taking of pledges is merely a means of pressure, designed to make a debtor live up to his obligations. The device has close parallels in the Bible,[2] and in Egyptian sources;[3] it is reminiscent also of the Roman *pignoris capio*.[4]

---

[1] Concerning deeds of submission, see also Seidl, *Einführung*, p. 38, *Rechtsgeschichte*, p. 38.

[2] Deuteronomy 24. 10–13.

[3] e.g. P. British Museum 10113 (568 B.C.), P. Louvre 9293 (499 B.C.).

[4] Cf. Seidl, *Rechtsgeschichte*, pp. 57 f.

IV

The Law of Persons

I. *Slavery*

SLAVERY is one of the topics on which the Elephantine documents yield interesting information. Indeed, we find a good deal even on matters not illuminated by the Egyptian sources.

In C 28 two sons of Mivṭaḥiah divide between them the slaves who had belonged to their mother. Each son of Mivṭaḥiah receives one son of the slave-woman Tebo. The woman herself and another son of hers remain for the time being in common ownership. Their assignment is postponed 'till it will be time', probably when the boy is grown up.[1]

The name of their owner, Mivṭaḥiah, is tattooed on the right arm of each of the two slaves, for the obvious purpose of making pursuit and identification easier should they make a bid for freedom by attempting to escape. Similar tattoo-marks are mentioned also in the description of Tamut, in her deed of manumission, K 5.[2]

One born as a slave is usually referred to by the name of his mother. In law only the freeborn has a father. Hence in C 28, the slaves assigned to the two sons of Mivṭaḥiah are described as sons of Tebo, their mother. In K 8 the child adopted is the son of *Tḥw'*, an Egyptian female name. In fact, wherever a man is referred to by his mother's name this gives rise to the presumption that he either is a slave, or was one but has been manumitted. So in K 12: 21 the two sailor brothers, Peḥi and Pemeṭ, whose house borders on the property sold by Anani b. Azariah, are called the sons of Tawi. Probably they were freedmen, though we shall see that the mere fact of their owning

---

[1] See already Cowley, p. 103.

[2] Cf. also Driver, Letter 7: 7. See, for the Babylonian practice, Driver and Miles, pp. 306 ff.; A. L. Oppenheim, *Bulletin of the American Schools of Oriental Research*, xciii (1944), p. 14. For Talmudic law, cf. Tosefta Makkoth 4. 15.

property does not rule out the possibility that they were still slaves. On the same ground Kraeling suggests that Berechiah b. Mifṭaḥ, a witness in K 5, also was a freedman. K 12: 3 is contrary to the general trend. Here the patronymic of Tamut is given. In Kraeling's view this may indicate that she was freeborn, and had subsequently become enslaved.[1]

It is usual for a person writing a letter to someone who is his superior in class or rank to describe himself as the 'slave' or 'servant' of the addressee.[2] This is, of course, nothing but a form of courtesy, which should not be taken to be of any legal import. In K 6: 8 one Ḥor is styled 'aved—'slave', 'servant' of Khnum. In other documents the same individual is referred to as 'gardener of Khnum the god' (K 9: 10, 10: 6). Here again it would be rash to assume actual slavery, even temple-slavery. Full freedom and service to a god are not necessarily incompatible.

The nature of a slave as a piece of property owned by his master is evident in the deeds of loan, C 10, K 11. In both of them slaves and slave-women ('aved wa'amah) are mentioned among chattels liable to seizure by the creditor in case he is not paid.

Outside the Elephantine documents one might refer to Driver, Letter 3, concerning the punishment of runaway slaves. Their owner applies to the Persian satrap: 'Now, if it be good to my lord, let (word) be sent unto 'Artawant[3] [that, if] I present [these men] before him, the punishment which I shall give orders to inflict upon them be inflicted upon them.' The request is granted. It should not be deduced from this letter that generally masters were restricted in the exercise of their domestic power over their slaves. It is rather that in the present case the writer was holding his property from the satrap,[4] a fact which might impose various limitations upon his freedom of action.

---

[1] At p. 275; see also his remarks at pp. 187, 224.
[2] See, for example, C 30: 1, 37: 1, K 13: 9; in contrast, equals address each other as 'brothers', e.g. C 40: 5: 'To my brother Pal[ṭi b. Yeo]sh thy brother Hoshaiah b. Nathan.'
[3] The satrap's representative in Egypt.
[4] See Driver, Letter 2.

Our main source of information concerning slavery is the archive of Anani b. Azariah. His wife Tamut, whom he married in 449 B.C. (K 2), was the slave-girl of Meshullam b. Zakkur. The document establishes the capacity of a slave for marriage, entered upon in a written contract. For all its meagreness of detail, K 2 corresponds in the main to other marriage contracts.[1] Tamut brings modest belongings into her marriage, but we do not know whether they had been her own before or were only provided by her master (or some other person) on this auspicious occasion. At any rate, it is clear that contrary, for example, to Roman law the fact that the bride is unfree does not preclude a legally valid marriage. On the other hand, marriage does not imply her release from slavery;[2] this emerges from K 5, Tamut's deed of manumission, executed twenty-two years after her marriage, in 427 B.C.

In K 4 (434 B.C.) Anani gives his wife part of a house. This shows that an unfree person may be the bearer of property rights, and that acquisitions of his do not automatically vest in the master.

K 2 contains provisions in contemplation of the death of the spouses. It follows that a slave is capable of passing on property *mortis causa*. However, the master is party to K 2; possibly he was legally entitled to the belongings of his deceased slave, and the arrangement depended upon his assent.[3]

K 5 (427 B.C.) is the deed of manumission of Tamut and of her daughter Yehoyishma. But it is to have effect only at the death of the manumitter, Meshullam b. Zakkur (*āzāta *šiv-qethki bemothi—'free have I relinquished thee at my death').[4] Yehoyishma is unquestionably the daughter of Anani b. Azariah,[5] none the less the manumitter refers to her as having been born to him. Apparently he is 'thinking not in terms of

---

[1] For divergences see pp. 47, 57, below.

[2] *Pace* Volterra, 'Affrancazioni', pp. 687 f., and cf. 'Identities', p. 351. It does, according to a minority opinion, in Talmudic law (Babylonian Talmud, Giṭṭin 40a); also in the law of Justinian, Codex 7. 6. 1. 9 (A.D. 531).

[3] See p. 70, below.

[4] On the meaning of *āzāta see, for example, J. de Menasce, *Bibliotheca Orientalis*, xi (1954), p. 161.

[5] Cf., for example, K 4: 18, and see generally 'Identities', p. 347.

paternity but of ownership'.[1] It is fairly certain that Yehoyishma was born during Tamut's marriage (she is not mentioned
in K 2, whereas Palṭi son of Tamut is), yet she is the property
of her mother's master. By giving his slave-woman in marriage
to a free person he had not relinquished his rights to her off-
spring.

To express manumission, in addition to the formula quoted,
'free have I relinquished thee . . .', use is made also of other
phrases: 'Thou art relinquished from shadow to sun' ('*anti
ševiqah min ṭulla' lesimša*'); this formula has parallels in later
Jewish sources.[2] Of a different type is 'thou art relinquished to
the god' ('*anti ševiqah le'elaha*'); this implies putting the manu-
mittee under the protection of the deity.[3]

Manumission does not, however, spell the immediate end of
any relationship between the manumitter and the person freed.
The two women are to continue to serve the manumitter 'as a
son or a daughter provides for his father'. Strictly speaking this
provision would seem superfluous, since by the terms of the
document the effect of the manumission is delayed till the death
of the manumitter. Maybe the parties intend to indicate that
even though legally slaves, the two women are in fact to enjoy
a considerable measure of freedom. Or else, seeing that the
women undertake to render these services to the manumitter's
son Zakkur, the provision in favour of the father may have been
inserted in a mechanical fashion. The undertaking of Tamut and
Yehoyishma resembles the παραμονή provisions usual in Greek
manumissions,[4] and is also paralleled in early Oriental sources.[5]
Both the promise not to attack the freedom of the two women
and the faithful discharge of the obligations undertaken by
them, are secured by penal stipulations amounting to 50 karsh
(= 500 shekels). These are among the biggest penalties stipulated in Elephantine.

[1] Kraeling, p. 178.
[2] Mishnah Pesaḥim 10. 5, Babylonian Talmud Kethuboth 112*b*; see Z. W. Falk,
Journal of Jewish Studies, v (1954), p. 116; Ginsberg, p. 158.
[3] See Rabinowitz, p. 33.
[4] So already Kraeling, p. 186; there are similar arrangements also in Roman
law (*operae liberti*); see M. Kaser, *Das römische Privatrecht*, i (1955), pp. 257 f.
[5] Rabinowitz, pp. 26 f.

The continued dependence of the freedwomen upon their patron and his son is illustrated also by the fact that in K 7, of 420 B.C., it is Zakkur b. Meshullam, who gives away Yehoyishma, here styled his 'sister'. Anani b. Azariah has no legal standing in the matter, though he gives his daughter some land, apparently on the occasion of her marriage (K 6). It has been suggested that manumission involved adoption by the manumitter,[1] and this would explain how the same Yehoyishma is at the same time the daughter of Anani and Tamut, and the sister of Zakkur, the son of her manumitter. In K 12: 11, 24, the latest of the documents belonging to the archive of Anani b. Azariah, reference is once more made to Tamut's former subjection to Meshullam b. Zakkur. She is called his *pedift (or *perift),[2] his former *gawwa'; the meaning of both these terms is not clear.[3]

II. *Adoption*

K 8, the only one of Kraeling's documents not belonging to the archive of Anani, is a deed of adoption. The circumstances of the transaction are quite obscure; possibly it is connected with some manumission.[4] The facts are briefly these: Zakkur b. Meshullam had by deed transferred a slave of his, Yedoniah b. *Thw'*, to one Uriah b. Maḥseiah. The latter now adopts Yedoniah: 'My son shall he be', and promises the payment of a penalty of 30 karsh in case his re-enslavement be attempted. By being made Uriah's son, Yedoniah would probably also acquire some claim to the inheritance of his adoptive father, although no mention is made of this point.[5]

It should be noted that the matter is arranged in the presence of the Persian commander of the garrison, a fact which points to some sort of participation of the authorities in the transaction.

---

[1] H. Cazelles, *Syria*, xxxii (1955), p. 80; Rabinowitz, p. 29.

[2] See p. 2, above, on the interchangeability of *d* and *r*.

[3] Various attempts at interpretation fail to carry conviction.

[4] See Volterra, 'Affrancazioni', p. 696. This has been more pronouncedly urged also by Z. W. Falk, JSS iii (1958), pp. 127 f.

[5] See Kraeling, pp. 55, 225.

The only other document described as executed in the presence of the commander is C 25, a deed of 'removal', probably written after litigation.

III. *Patria Potestas*

The papyri convey no information as to the extent of a father's authority over his children. In C 15 the father of the bride gives her away in marriage, but in K 7, we have seen, the father has to concede this right to the son of the manumitter. In C 18 it is probable that the bride is given away by the mother, possibly because the father is dead. It is difficult to discern the substantive import of this giving away of a bride. It may indeed be a mere survival from an earlier period.[1] The person giving away the bride does get the brideprice, but it has been shown that the sum paid by the bridegroom is handed back to the couple.[2] This too probably reflects a development: in earlier times, one may assume, the payment was kept by the person receiving it.

The children of a debtor are bound to pay his debts and their property is liable to seizure under the provisions of the deeds of loan C 10, K 11. But this has its basis in the rules of succession, rather than in those of *potestas*. In C 10 the borrower is a woman and it is highly questionable whether a woman could have *potestas* at all. In K 11 the obligation of meeting the debts of the deceased is imposed not only upon his children, but also upon his *'adrang*, relatives of some kind (perhaps 'heirs'?) but obviously persons outside *potestas*.

In this context it is also to be noted that K 11 does not concede the creditor the power to seize the persons of his debtor's children. They are indeed obliged to pay the debt, but are not liable to seizure. Herein the Aramaic practice differs distinctly from the demotic one: there the list of objects liable to seizure as pledges usually includes also *šry šr.t*—'son, daughter'.[3] How-

---

[1] See pp. 45 f., below.
[2] Ginsberg, p. 156; cf. p. 48, below.
[3] See, for example, P. British Museum 10113 (568 B.C.), P. Louvre 9293 (499 B.C.); cf. Seidl, *Rechtsgeschichte*, p. 49.

ever, it is not desired to suggest that this is proof of a real difference in the extent of the father's power. Firstly, our material is much too limited to warrant a conclusion (there is no reference to any kind of pledge in the third deed of loan, C 11). Secondly, even Egyptian practice was not completely uniform: there is at least one demotic deed, P. Berlin 3110 (488 B.C.), which does not make the debtor's children liable to seizure. Finally, the power of pledging one's children is evidenced in contemporary Judaea (as is shown by the narrative in Nehemiah 5. 1 ff.), and in Neo-Babylonian deeds of loan. There are no plausible grounds for holding that the Elephantine practice concerning the pledging of one's children was in advance of all other contemporary systems.

IV. *Women*

The position of women in Elephantine compares favourably with that in other parts of the ancient Near East. This will become clear especially when the law of marriage and divorce is considered in detail. Persian influence has been invoked,[1] but with little apparent justification, even if only because our knowledge of Persian law is so limited.[2] It seems rather that one ought to look to Egyptian law for an explanation.

In the law of procedure we already noted that women at Elephantine do not attest documents. The situation in this respect is not different from contemporary demotic practice.[3] But they can be parties to litigation, and are capable of taking an oath. This is evidenced by C 6, where the wife of the defendant, Maḥseiah b. Yedoniah, joins him in denying the allegation of the plaintiff, and by C 14, where Mivṭaḥiah is a direct party to the litigation and wins the case by taking an oath by the Egyptian goddess Sati.

In the field of the law of property and obligations we find women enjoying full equality. They go about their transactions in the same manner as men, and no trace of inferiority or male

[1] U. Türck, *Zeitschrift für die alttestamentliche Wissenschaft*, xlvi (1928), pp. 166 ff.
[2] See Kutscher, p. 247, and the literature adduced there.
[3] See Seidl, *Rechtsgeschichte*, p. 50.

supervision of any kind is discernible. Their capacity of owning property is evidenced by the numerous deeds of gift (in all of which women are the donees, a fact which may be of significance with regard to the rules of succession); also by the deeds concerning barter (C 1, 43), and by the marriage contracts which provide for the return to the divorcee of the dowry which she has brought with her. In loans we find women both as debtor (C 10) and as creditor (C 35).

Several of the documents are executed by women: so C 1 and 43, both concerning barter, and the deed of loan C 10; the fragmentary marriage contract C 18 is apparently dictated by the bridegroom and the mother of the bride. In this connexion it is of interest that the bride is not a party to the marriage contract, even though this confers considerable rights upon her. Formally the parties to the marriage contract are the bridegroom and the head of the family of the bride. We shall have more to say on this matter in the next chapter.

In the field of succession women may have been in an inferior position. We shall discuss this in due course.[1]

Outside the sphere of private law, we may observe that women are apparently enlisted in the military units which made up the population of Elephantine. This seems probable from C 14, K 3, and from the fragmentary C 43.[2] Equality of property rights also involves the duty to share in the burden of taxation. In C 22 women are conspicuous among the contributors to the temple fund, paying 2 shekels each, just like the men.

---

[1] See pp. 67 f., below.   [2] See Cowley, p. xvii.

V

Marriage and Divorce

OUR main source for the law of marriage and divorce are the three marriage contracts C 15, K 2 and 7. C 15 (= Sayce and Cowley's Papyrus G) aroused much interest in its time. The first to comment on it, in a review published in 1906,[1] was M. Lidzbarski, who called it a *regelrechte Kethubah*, that is, a proper Jewish marriage contract, as known from the Talmudic and later periods. This description has been uncritically adopted by many scholars.[2] In actual fact, all that connects C 15 (and the other two marriage contracts from Elephantine) with the Talmudic *kethubah* is the common subject matter, marriage. It is almost inevitable that some of the points dealt with should be identical. There is no similarity going farther than this, and even if there were agreement in the way these points are regulated, it would still not prove any contact between the Elephantine marriage contracts and their Talmudic counterpart.[3]

The three Aramaic marriage contracts have certain basic features in common, but there is not complete uniformity. With regard to K 2, the unfree status of the bride will occasionally be of significance and must always be borne in mind. It may be best to consider first the conclusion of marriage, to turn next to the pecuniary aspects, i.e. the dowry and the rules concerning matrimonial property, and to end with the dissolution of marriage.

---

[1] *Deutsche Literaturzeitung*, 1906, col. 3205–15; it is reprinted in *Ephemeris für semitische Epigraphik*, iii (1909–15), pp. 70–81.

[2] e.g. L. Freund, *Wiener Zeitschrift für die Kunde des Morgenlandes*, xxi (1907), p. 170; S. Jampel, *Monatsschrift für Geschichte und Wissenschaft des Judentums*, li (1907), p. 619; L. Blau, *Magyar-Zsidó Szemle*, xxiv (1907), p. 225; J. N. Epstein, *Jahrbuch der jüdisch-literarischen Gesellschaft*, vi (1908), p. 365.

[3] See p. 100, below.

I. *The Conclusion of Marriage*

Marriage comes about by several steps, each of which has to be considered separately. These are (*a*) the bridegroom's request that the bride be given to him; (*b*) a declaration by the bridegroom that the bride is his wife and he is her husband; (*c*) the payment of the brideprice, the *mohar*;[1] (*d*) the drawing up of a written marriage contract.

(*a*) The bridegroom addresses the head of the family of the bride. He declares that he has come to ask for the bride. 'I have come to thy house that thou mightest give to me X thy daughter in wifehood.'[2] The phrasing reflects the position of the bridegroom as a supplicant, desirous of the acceptance of his request, of the assent of the bride's father. In one document, K 7, the bridegroom adds that his request has been acceded to ('thou hast given her to me'), in the others this is a necessary implication. No doubt, the person giving away the bride is usually her father (*stricto sensu*), but it so happens that the few documents which we have show a great variety of possibilities. Only in C 15 is it actually the father of the bride. In K 2 Tamut, bride and slave-girl, is given away by her master; in K 7 it is the son of her manumitter, to whom she is bound by a παραμονή agreement, who gives away the bride, here described as his 'sister'. In C 18 it is probably the mother of the bride who gives her away, but owing to the state of the document one cannot be sure about this.

It appears, then, that in the Elephantine documents marriage is a legal transaction the parties to which are the bridegroom and the head of the family of the bride. At least from the formal legal point of view it is not an agreement between the bridegroom and the bride. The contracts contain no expression of her assent, which at an earlier time may have been irrelevant, in law at least if not in fact. On the other hand, it looks as if the assent of the person having *potestas* over the bride is essential for the conclusion of a lawful marriage, that is to say, he looks like

---

[1] The Hebrew vocalization is used, since the Aramaic is quite uncertain, **mehar* or **muhura*.

[2] The phrase is not completely stereotyped. For slight variations see 'Marriage Contracts', pp. 4, 29.

having a power of veto. Yet we cannot be confident that this is still the case in the middle of the fifth century B.C., at the time of these documents. Agreements of this kind are apt to retain the traditional phrasing of a remote past, in disregard of far-reaching changes which have taken place in actual life. Our doubts are accentuated by the Egyptian material: in early marriage contracts the transaction is one between the bridegroom and the father of the bride,[1] just as in Elephantine. But a significant change takes place late in the Saitic period: the agreement is now concluded between the bridegroom and the bride.[2] However, the decisive point, and about this there is no doubt, is that the wife in Elephantine is her husband's equal as far as the power of unilateral divorce is concerned. Once such a power is recognized, at least *de facto* assent of the bride to her marriage must inevitably be required. To sum up: the situation is one of material equality disguised as formal inferiority.[3]

(*b*) The bridegroom's request (*a*) is followed by his declaration, identical in all the contracts: 'She is my wife and I am her husband . . .'. A party's assertion of the existence of a certain legal relationship, his 'acknowledging' it, is creative of that relationship.[4] This is ancient Eastern practice, to be encountered not only, as here, in the context of marriage (and divorce), but also in other spheres, e.g. adoption of a child and dismission of a child (natural or adopted) from the family.

In this double phrase the first part, 'she is my wife', is the important one, as may be seen from the introduction (*a*), speaking of wifehood only, and from the divorce formulas, as given in K 7: 'I divorce X my wife, she shall not be to me a

---

[1] See P. Berlin 3048 verso (probably of 879 B.C.), P. Cairo 30907+30909 (676 B.C.?), P. Louvre 7849 (589 B.C.), and P. Louvre 7846 (546 B.C.). The documents are now conveniently available, in transliteration and German translation, in E. Lüddeckens, *Ägyptische Eheverträge*, 1960. (Documents 1–4.)

[2] First in P. Berlin 13614 (535 B.C.?) = Lüddeckens no. 5.

[3] In Talmudic law the contract is between the bridegroom and the bride, and the assent of the bride is essential; see, e.g., Babylonian Talmud Qiddushin 2*b*.

[4] Cf. D. Daube, *Studies in Biblical Law*, 1947, pp. 7 f., for ample documentation. See also Seidl, *Rechtsgeschichte*, p. 25, who, following Daube, speaks of a *persönliche Anerkennungsurkunde*.

wife', and 'I divorce thee, I shall not be to thee a wife'. The addition '. . . and I am her husband' does indicate an element of mutuality, but exactly what legal consequences are attached to it is doubtful.[1]

The bridegroom's declaration is concluded by the words 'from this day and for ever' (K 2, C 15), or 'from this day for ever' (K 7, 14). This phrase is not peculiar to marriage contracts. It occurs in other types of documents, and is frequent especially in conveyances, e.g. 'thou hast power over it from this day for ever'. It does not imply the indissolubility of the marriage; this is obvious from the detailed provisions concerning divorce contained in these contracts. Similarly, in conveyances containing the same phrase the right of the buyer to alienate what he has acquired is frequently stressed. Nor, it is submitted, need the phrase in the present context be regarded as an expression of sentiment, a pious wish that the marriage be a lasting one; at any rate such a connotation would be additional to its primary meaning. What 'from this day and for ever' primarily means is that the legal relationship in question is not *a priori* limited in time. Hence the phrase is used in sale, but it would be inappropriate in a lease for a term of years. It might occur in a release, but not in a pact not to sue during a certain period.[2]

(*c*) In accordance with general Eastern custom, marriage involves the payment by the bridegroom of a brideprice (*mohar*) to the head of the bride's family. The sums paid as *mohar* vary from document to document. Five shekels are paid in C 15, 1 karsh (= 10 shekels) in K 7. In K 2 no mention is made of a *mohar*. Ginsberg has carefully considered this question and has come to the conclusion that in K 2 the *mohar* amounts to $7\frac{1}{2}$ shekels.[3] We shall return to this point,[4] and shall submit that possibly in K 2 no *mohar* properly so called is paid at all,

---

[1] The Babylonian Talmud, Qiddushin 5*b*, rejects 'I am thy husband' (by itself) as a marriage formula.

[2] Cf., on 'from this day and for ever', S. E. Loewenstamm, *Israel Exploration Journal*, vi (1956), pp. 221 f.

[3] See his detailed argument at p. 156 of his article.

[4] See p. 57, below.

in other words that the omission of any reference to it is not accidental.

We should like to know whether the amount of the *mohar* was regulated, to some extent at least, by law or custom, or was entirely dependent upon the pleasure of the parties. For the time being no answer can be given. The variations in the three contracts become less significant once one recalls that there are special circumstances in each case: in C 15 the bride was a divorcee, in K 7 a freedwoman. The absence of any *mohar* in K 2, we shall suggest, may be due to the slave-status of the bride.

In both C 15 and K 7 the *mohar* is included in the dowry.[1] That means that the nominal recipient of the brideprice derives no actual benefit from it. There is evidence for such a practice of returning the brideprice already in the Old-Babylonian marriage documents.[2] Recently its occurrence has been demonstrated also in a fifteenth-century tablet from Alalakh.[3] This practice is of interest, since it foreshadows the future line of development. Once it has become a general custom that the father of the bride returns to her the brideprice, to be included in her dowry, the payment of the *mohar* will in due course become a fiction, with practical consequences only if and when the marriage is terminated.

(*d*) The three particulars so far mentioned are recorded in the marriage contract: the request of the bridegroom that the bride be given to him, his constitutive declaration, the statement that the *mohar* has been paid to the satisfaction of the father of the bride. It is difficult to decide whether the writing down of these particulars is an *essentiale negotii*, a fourth requirement, as indispensable for the conclusion of a lawful marriage as the other three acts themselves, or whether the document is merely a means of proof, both in respect of these particulars and in respect of any other provisions contained in it. That a written

---

[1] See Cowley, pp. xxx f. for C 15, Ginsberg, ibid., for K 7. Ginsberg suggests the same also for K 2; see p. 57, below.

[2] UAZP, no. 209; J. Kohler and A. Ungnad, *Hammurabis Gesetz*, iii (1909), texts 9, 10. All the three documents are available also in Driver and Miles, pp. 253 ff.

[3] Text 92; see I. Mendelsohn, 'Marriage in Alalakh', *Essays on Jewish Life and Thought Presented in Honor of S. W. Baron*, 1959, pp. 352 f.

marriage contract was essential in some systems, at least, of the ancient East is clear, for example, from sec. 28 of the Laws of Eshnunna, and sec. 128 of the Code of Hammurabi. Though there are differences of opinion concerning the exact function of the written marriage contract, scholars are agreed that it was very widely used.[1]

While not dissenting from the prevalent view, I am not sure whether it holds true also for Elephantine. The main reason for doubt is that, contrary to general Eastern practice, there is in the Bible absolutely no evidence for a marriage contract in writing, a fact which has not escaped the notice of scholars. Many actual cases of marriage are related in detail, marriage between God and Israel is a frequent symbolical theme of the prophets, but writing is not mentioned. Though, as a rule, much reliance should not be put upon arguments from silence, it seems plausible enough that the written marriage contract was not the common practice in pre-exilic Judaea.[2]

If that is so, we must assume that in reducing their marriage agreements to writing the colonists at Elephantine followed either the practice generally obtaining (as we have just seen) in the ancient East, or that of their Egyptian neighbours. Which of the two possible sources of influence was the one actually operative, we cannot know for certain; but if, as we think, the colonists at the time of their immigration into Egypt did not yet write marriage contracts, it would seem more likely that they subsequently adopted the practice of their neighbours. In support one might refer to the fact that the phrase introducing the contracts, 'I have come to thy house . . .', is typical of early Egyptian marriage contracts.[3]

However, the view that the inhabitants of Judaea and the

[1] See, for example, Driver and Miles, pp. 245 ff.; A. Van Praag, *Droit Matrimoniel assyro-babylonien*, 1945, pp. 84 ff. Mendelsohn (loc. cit., p. 351) defines marriage in the ancient Near East as 'a civil affair based on a written contract'.

[2] Others hold differently. For a more detailed discussion of the point see 'Marriage Contracts', pp. 36 f.

[3] For the Egyptian phrase, *'k r pr*, cf. Lüddeckens, p. 8, note 2. It occurs already in the 'Adoption Papyrus', of the twelfth century B.C., published by A. H. Gardiner, JEA xxvi (1940), pp. 23 ff. For later periods, see the documents mentioned in note 1, p. 46, above.

founders of the colony at Elephantine probably did not reduce their marriage agreements to writing does not imply that marriage was essentially informal. Forms may be observed in oral transactions no less strictly than in writing. Actually, such oral forms have been preserved in the Elephantine documents. They were, in the case of marriage, 'she is my wife and I am her husband, from this day and for ever'; and in divorce, as we shall see, 'I divorce X my wife, she shall not be unto me a wife'.

II. *Dowry and Matrimonial Property*

All three marriage contracts give detailed lists of the chattels brought into the marriage by the bride. There are various items; first of all there is a sum of money (12 shekels in C 15, slightly more than 22 shekels in K 7), called *kesaf tekhunah*, the exact meaning of which term is not clear. To this is to be added the *mohar*, with which, we may recall, the bride is also credited. There follow pieces of clothing, various objects for the personal use of the bride, as well as household utensils, each with its price stated. All these items are added up, to give— together with the cash and the *mohar*—the total value of the dowry. Each of the contracts mentions also various items of apparently minor importance, on which no value is put.[1] The list of belongings is drawn up in contemplation of divorce, details of which we shall consider in due course.

It should be noted that these lists do not comprise all the property of the bride; immoveables belonging to her are not here accounted for. We know that in 447 B.C. Mivṭaḥiah's father conveyed a house to her (C 13), but in her marriage contract (C 15, of 441 B.C. or later) no reference is made to it; yet it is fairly probable that she did not alienate the house, or else the deed of conveyance would not have remained in her archive but would have been handed over to the alienee.[2] Similarly, Yehoyishma was given a house in July 420 B.C. (K 6), but no reference is made to it in her marriage contract (K 7), drawn up some three months later. It seems then that the need

[1] Cf. Ginsberg, p. 156, note 4.
[2] For the practice of transferring old title-deeds, see p. 31, above.

to safeguard the rights of the wife was not felt in the case of land, where there were other documents, deeds of sale or gift, to prove her title.

Occasionally the dowry may have been provided by the bride herself; so apparently in C 15, recording the third marriage of Mivṭaḥiah, who would already have had opportunity to accumulate a good deal of property. More often the chattels, or at least the money, would be provided by the head of the bride's family; so both in C 18 and K 7. In these documents the giver of the dowry renounces any future claim to it. If he will try to base himself upon the fact that the giving of the dowry was without consideration (beraḥamin)—no attention shall be paid to him.[1]

We should like to know whether the dowry was thought of as passing into the ownership of the bridegroom, or whether it was rather considered the property of the wife. The language of the contracts is not quite decisive, but on the whole the former construction, ownership of the bridegroom, seems preferable. His ownership may indeed have been largely onerous, entailing liability in case of destruction or deterioration, without a right to alienate or even to deprive the wife of the use of the chattel, but it is ownership all the same. There are suggestive linguistic indications: first there is the bridegroom's declaration that the bride has brought in 'to him' such and such chattels, or that she has brought them 'to his house'. Perhaps of greater legal significance is the acknowledgement by the bridegroom in C 15: 15: 'his heart is satisfied' with the dowry brought by the wife. The same phrase occurs in receipts of sums of money, for example, where a purchase price is paid. On general grounds, if money was handed to the bridegroom, to be spent by him, we must assume that it passed into his ownership.

It is tempting to see an essential difference between such objects as are listed in the marriage contract, and such as are not: the former do pass into the ownership of the husband who thereby becomes liable for them; the latter remain outside the arrangement and are unaffected by the husband-and-wife

[1] Concerning the dowry of Tamut (K 2), see p. 38, above.

relationship obtaining between the parties. The management of the wife's property might be in the hands of the husband even though it is not listed in the contract. Such management need not, *per se*, render him liable in case of loss or deterioration.

An interesting stipulation concerning matrimonial property occurs in C 15. The husband declares that he will not be entitled to take away his goods and possessions from his wife. If he acts in contravention of this undertaking, he will have to pay a penalty of 200 shekels. This means, in essence, that the wife has to concur in the alienations of any property by her husband. Her dissent could not indeed invalidate the transaction, but the penalty clause would be a sufficient safeguard.[1]

This raises the more general question of the property relationship between the spouses, a question on which there are differences of opinion between various scholars. Some hold that the matrimonial régime was one of community of goods between the spouses,[2] others that the property interests of husband and wife were separate.[3] Apparently it would be going too far to speak of a 'community of goods'. If this were the rule, the gift of half a house by a husband to his wife (K 4) would make little sense. But the general test is the case of divorce. There is nothing to suggest the existence of any common property, to be divided up between the spouses in the event of the marriage being dissolved.[4] On the other hand, as long as the marriage subsisted, the provision in C 15 gave the wife a recognized position, a *Beispruchsrecht*, with respect to the property of the husband. This was obviously useful, to ensure both the continued material basis for the marriage, and the husband's ability to meet his obligations in case the marriage was dissolved.[5] Arrangements

---

[1] See, however, p. 61, below.   [2] See Rabinowitz, p. 63.

[3] E. Bickermann, RIDA iii (1956), p. 87.

[4] Such arrangements occur in some demotic marriage contracts. See, for example, P. British Museum 10120A, of 517 B.C. (Lüddeckens no. 6): the divorcee wife is to get one-third of all common acquisitions; so also in P. Lonsdorfer, of 363 B.C. (Lüddeckens no. 8). In P. Philadelphia 875 B, of 264 B.C. (Lüddeckens no. 13) she is promised one-half.

[5] The clause is not a freak: this is shown by the occurrence of similar provisions in some Greco-Egyptian marriage contracts: P. Giessen 2: 23 (173 B.C.), and P. Tebtunis 104: 22 (92 B.C.).

concerning the devolution of property in case of the death of a spouse are considered in the next chapter.[1]

III. *The Dissolution of Marriage*

In the Elephantine documents divorce is one of the more difficult topics. Although the main points are clear enough, various details have given rise to a number of theories which have proved untenable. One such defunct theory is that of 'illegal expulsion';[2] another is that of 'divorce by conduct'.[3]

All three marriage contracts contain provisions concerning divorce. Each considers, in separate clauses, divorce at the initiative of the husband and divorce at the initiative of the wife. The most interesting feature of divorce at Elephantine is the equal capacity of the spouses, as far as the power of dissolution of the marriage is concerned. This is in striking contrast to the situation which on the whole obtains in the ancient East,[4] and also in Talmudic law, where the husband alone is entitled to dissolve the marriage (the only mitigation being the court's power to bring pressure to bear upon him to divorce).[5] The equality at Elephantine is probably due to the Egyptian environment.

In K 2 and 7 divorce on the initiative of the husband is considered first, and one might regard this as the sequence to be expected; yet this need not be so: C 15 has the inverted order. Each of the two clauses refers to three stages of divorce: (*a*) one of the two spouses will utter a declaration of divorce; (*b*) certain payments will fall due between the spouses; finally (*c*) the wife will have to leave the matrimonial home. As an example we may quote the two clauses from C 15: 22 ff.:

[1] See pp. 69 ff., below.
[2] See pp. 73 f., below.
[3] Suggested in 'Marriage Contracts', pp. 23 f.; differently in JSS v (1960), p. 69. I have now altogether abandoned the concept. See pp. 61 f., below.
[4] See, e.g. on Babylonian and biblical law, Driver and Miles, pp. 290 ff. But there are instances in which a wife's power to divorce the husband appears to be admitted. See, e.g. Hrozny, Kültepe no. 3 (*Symbolae Koschaker*, 1939, p. 109), and the marriage contracts from Alalakh, discussed by Mendelsohn (loc. cit.).
[5] See, for example, Mishnah Kethuboth 7. 9, 10; Arakhin 5. 6.

Divorce on the initiative of the wife:

(a) *Declaration of divorce*: Tomorrow [or] another day, (if) [Miv]ṭaḥiah should stand up in the congregation and say, 'I divorce Asḥor my husband' . . .

(b) *Provisions relating to property*: . . . divorce money is on her head; she shall put upon the scales and weigh out to [As]ḥor silver 7 shekels 2R, and all that she brought in in her hand she shall take out, both shred (?) and thread . . .

(c) *Departure from the matrimonial home*: . . . and she shall go away whither she will, and no suit or process (shall obtain).

Divorce on the initiative of the husband:

(a) *Declaration of divorce*: Tomorrow or another day, (if) Asḥor should stand up in the congregation and say, 'I divorce my [wi]fe Mivṭaḥiah' . . .

(b) *Provisions relating to property*: . . . her *mohar* [shall] be lost, and all that she brought in in her hand she shall take out, both shred (?) and thread, on one day at one time . . .

(c) *Departure from the matrimonial home*: . . . and she shall go away whither she will, and no suit or process (shall obtain).

The declaration of divorce is similar in all three contracts, though there are minor variations. The party initiating the divorce is 'standing up in the congregation'. In K 2 and 7 only the husband is referred to as doing so, the wife simply as making the declaration, but no importance should be attached to this. The wife's equal capacity to make the declaration *coram publico* is attested by C 15. Divorce requires certainty and publicity. In Deuteronomic law (24. 1) certainty is assured by the delivery of a bill of divorce to the wife, but no such document is mentioned in the Aramaic papyri. Admittedly, the material at our disposal is not large enough to allow a safe conclusion, but it seems probable that the writing of bills of divorce was not the practice at Elephantine, or else they would occur in the detailed description of divorce formalities. As the proper formula had to be spoken 'in the congregation', both the need for certainty and that for publicity were satisfied.[1] The congregation had no other function in the matter; in particular no judicial function ought to be attributed to it.

The verb rendered above by 'to divorce' is *śena'*, the literal meaning of which is 'to hate': 'I hate thee', or, objectively, 'I hate X, my wife (Y, my husband)'. Originally this may have expressed merely the motive for divorce, to be followed by a further statement actually abolishing the relationship between the spouses. We find such more detailed formulas in K 7: there, after declaring 'hatred', the divorcing spouse goes on, 'she shall not be to me a wife', or 'I shall not be to thee a wife', as the case may be. These additions are the converse of the formulas used in the declaration of marriage.[2] In spite of the fact that K 7 is the latest of the Elephantine marriage contracts, the fuller version preserved in it is apparently the earlier one. Support for this assumption is furnished by Hosea 2. 4: '. . . for she is not my wife, neither am I her husband.' At some stage, it seems, 'hatred' acquired the secondary, transferred meaning 'divorce', whereupon the *formula contraria* was occasionally dispensed with. The more pregnant meaning of *śena'* is evidenced also by such technical terms as *kesaf śin'ah*— 'money of divorce' (literally, 'silver of hatred'), and *din śin'ah*— 'law of divorce' (literally, 'of hatred'). The use of verbs meaning 'to hate' as terms of divorce in other sources will be discussed later.[3] Another term of divorce is *tarekh*—'to expel', equivalent to Hebrew *gereš*. In Elephantine it occurs only once in the context of divorce (K 2: 14), several times in its primary, non-technical meaning.

Nothing in the documents suggests that, for divorce to take place, in addition to the subjective desire of the parties, any objective cause was required. There was no need for any 'matrimonial offence', such as is required by various modern legal

---

[1] For further discussion, cf. 'Marriage Contracts', pp. 14 ff., also H. L. Ginsberg, JNES xviii (1959), pp. 148 f.

[2] See p. 46, above.

[3] See pp. 101 f., below.

systems (under the influence of Christianity's negative attitude
to divorce). Comparison with classical Roman law would be
more to the point. In Elephantine, just as in Rome, the con-
tinuation of a marriage depended upon the will of both the
spouses, each of whom enjoyed full power to dissolve it unilater-
ally. Technically there is no divorce by agreement: divorce is
unilateral even if proceeding from the joint desire of the spouses.[1]
All this does not mean that the factual background of the separation, the chain of events leading up to it, is always irrelevant.
The question 'who is to blame?' might be of significance when
the pecuniary consequences of the divorce were to be decided.
To this topic we are now passing.

We have seen that marriage had a considerable effect upon
the proprietary rights and liabilities of the spouses. So much is
certain even though many details are doubtful. It is only reasonable that divorce should be accompanied by the reversal, as far
as that is practicable, of the relationship created by the marriage. In addition, divorce was the occasion for other payments:
the party taking the initiative, or bearing the blame, might be
bound to pay *kesaf śin'ah*—'divorce money'. The sum payable
varies according to whether the husband or the wife was the
divorcing party.

As for the sum payable by a divorcing husband, the documents provide as follows:

C 15: 27 f.: . . . her *mohar* [shall] be lost, and all that she
brought in in her hand, she shall take out . . .

K 2: 8: . . . divorce money is on his head; he shall give
to Tamut silver 7 shekels 2R, and all that she
brought in in her hand, she shall take out . . .

K 7: 22 ff.: . . . divorce money is on his head; all that she
brought in into his house he shall give to her, her
substance, and her garments in the value of
silver karsh seven sh[ekels eight, ḥallur 5] and

---

[1] See, for classical Roman law, E. Levy, *Der Hergang der römischen Ehescheidung*,
1925, p. 76. There is, of course, the difference between the two, that in Rome
divorce was informal, whereas in Elephantine forms had to be observed, i.e. a set
formula had to be spoken in the congregation, but the importance of this difference
should not be exaggerated; it does not go to the root of the matter.

> the rest of the goods which are written (above)
> he shall give to her . . .

Ginsberg suggests that the divorce money is in this case
'simply the brideprice which he has nominally paid to her
guardian but which is actually added to her dowry'.[1] In his
view, then, the payment of the *mohar* is merely a fiction, just as
later in the Talmudic *kethubah*. While this interpretation is not
to be rejected out of hand,[2] I am not sure that it is the correct one.

It is plausible for C 15, but then this document does not mention
the divorce money, but merely states that 'her *mohar* shall be lost',
lost, that is, to the divorcing husband. Ginsberg's interpretation is
more doubtful in K 7, which has two distinct statements, (*a*) payment of divorce money, and (*b*) return of the dowry; under this head
(*b*) a sum of money is mentioned which includes also the *mohar*
originally given. It is difficult to regard the two provisions, (*a*) and
(*b*), as not cumulative.

Finally, this interpretation runs into trouble over the special case
of K 2, in which, it will be recalled, there is no reference to a payment of a *mohar*. But there are two other relevant data. The one is
the endorsement, on the back of the document: 'Tamut brought in
to Anani in her hand silver, one karsh, five shekels' (= 15 shekels).
This, however, exceeds by more than $7\frac{1}{2}$ shekels the amount given in
line 6 f. of the document as the value of Tamut's dowry. The other
relevant fact is the provision, in line 8, for the payment of $7\frac{1}{2}$ shekels
divorce money, in case Anani divorces Tamut. Ginsberg, equating
divorce money and *mohar*, holds that the latter amounted in K 2 to
$7\frac{1}{2}$ shekels. Thereby he disposes of the contradictions between the
endorsement and line 6, and also obtains a substitute for the *mohar*.

This, however, does not explain the omission, hardly accidental,
of a reference to the *mohar*. Moreover, it is only K 2 which names
the amount of divorce money payable by the divorcing husband.
The possibility arises that no *mohar*, in the strict sense of the term,
was paid, and this because of the unfree status of the bride; in other
words, the payment of a *mohar* appears as one of the characteristics
of the marriage of a free woman.

There is, however, every reason to assume that there was some
payment to Tamut's master, though it could not be *mohar*. The
exact amount of this must remain unknown. Only belatedly, after
the document was already sealed, may the master have been induced
to return the silver (all or part?) to the couple, as was customary in
the marriage of free people, and so the dowry increased to 15

---

[1] See p. 156 of his article.
[2] I accepted it in 'Marriage Contracts', pp. 16 ff.

shekels. We may mention that K 2 shows other signs of last-minute changes.[1]

The question, then, is: what sum would Anani have had to pay, had he divorced Tamut? Prima facie, the 15 shekels mentioned in the endorsement of K 2, plus the divorce money of $7\frac{1}{2}$ shekels.

If this is correct, Ginsberg's interpretation of K 2 and 7 is not, and we have to substitute a different one: there were two payments by the husband, the one at the time of the conclusion of the marriage, the other at the time of its dissolution. This interpretation has also the support of sources outside Elephantine:

First, there are the provisions of the Code of Hammurabi. Section 138 obliges a husband divorcing his first wife, who has not borne to him sons, to give her 'money to the value of her brideprice' (*mala terḫatiša*). Sections 139 and 140 fix the divorce money (*uzubbūm*) payable where there has been no brideprice. Of more immediate relevance is a series of demotic marriage contracts, beginning with P. Lonsdorfer, of 363 B.C., that is to say, quite close in time to the Elephantine papyri.[2] These contracts record two payments, the one at the conclusion of the marriage, the other at its dissolution; e.g., in P. Lonsdorfer, lines 1 f.: *Ich habe dich zu (meiner) Ehefrau gemacht, ich habe dir gegeben 5/10 Silberdeben . . . als deine Frauengabe. Wenn ich dich als Frau entlasse, . . . so gebe ich dir 5/10 Silberdeben, . . . abgesehen von jenen 5/10 Silberdeben, die oben verzeichnet sind, die ich dir als deine Frauengabe gegeben habe, so daß es zusammen ausmacht ein (ganzes) Silberdeben . . .* The first payment recorded in the documents may well have been fictitious, as various scholars suggest, but this does not affect our argument: at the time of divorce the husband was bound to pay both the sums.[3] Finally, we may mention that the rule of two payments obtains also in Karaite legal practice[4] and Islamic law ('prompt' and 'deferred' *mahr*).[5]

The divorce money payable by a repudiating wife amounts in all three documents to $7\frac{1}{2}$ shekels, though, we have seen, the amount of the *mohar* paid by the bridegroom is not constant. The figure of the divorce money may have been fixed by custom.

---

[1] See pp. 14, above, 70, below.

[2] Published by H. Junker, *Sitzungsberichte der Akademie der Wissenschaften in Wien*, 197 (1921), no. 2 (Lüddeckens no. 8); see also P. Philadelphia 875 B; P. Hauswaldt 4, 247–221 B.C. (Lüddeckens, no. 16), &c.

[3] The two sums are not always equal. For example, in P. Philadelphia 875B, the first payment amounts to 1 Deben, the second to 5, altogether 6. In P. Berlin 13593, 198 B.C. (see p. 73, note 1, below), the first payment amounts to 3 Deben, the second to 5, altogether 8.

[4] See S. Assaph, Supplement to *Tarbiz* i, 1930, p. 62 (Hebrew).

[5] See S. Vesey-Fitzgerald, *Muhammadan Law*, 1931, pp. 66 f.

Nevertheless, it appears that the three documents are not completely uniform in their provisions regarding the pecuniary consequences of divorce by the wife. In C 15, on payment of $7\frac{1}{2}$ shekels the repudiating wife is entitled to receive back her dowry, including the *mohar* paid (in fact or theory) by the husband. In K 2 she is probably entitled to the sum of 15 shekels mentioned in the endorsement. But the corresponding provision in K 7: 25 f. reads as follows: '... divorce money is on her head; her *mohar* shall be lost. She shall put upon the scales and give to her husband Ananiah silver, shekels 7, 2R ...'. In other words, not only has she to pay divorce money, but also her *mohar* is lost to her, it is to be deducted from the amount payable by the husband. Unfortunately, there is a gap in line 27, where the sum due from the husband was stated, so there can be no final certainty on this point.[1] It is not without interest that very similar provisions are laid down in the Alalakh marriage contract (text 92), to which we have already referred: in case of divorce by the wife she loses her *terḫatum* (= *mohar*); but if the husband divorces her, he has to pay up in full.[2]

The purpose of the payment of divorce money is not clear to me. The amount may be traditional, from earlier times, when it was more substantial (and the same may be true also of the *mohar*). In fifth-century Elephantine the sums involved are not large enough to be of much practical importance. As a basis for comparison we may mention that in K 2 a woollen garment is estimated at 7 shekels. Hence, the requirement that a wife must pay the cash-amount of $7\frac{1}{2}$ shekels as a first step in divorce can hardly have acted as a decisive restraint. On the other hand it seems that cash did not abound in Elephantine, as we can learn from the deeds of loan (C 10, 11, 35), all of which are for small sums (4 or 2 shekels). The husband has not only to pay divorce money, but is also bound to return the dowry; his obligations would probably restrain him more effectively from a rash divorce.

On divorce at the instance of either party, the wife is entitled to the dowry. It is for this purpose that the detailed valuation is

---

[1] See 'Marriage Contracts', pp. 17 f.
[2] See Mendelsohn, op. cit., pp. 352 f.

included in the marriage contract. At the time of divorce the objects used by the wife—whether initially brought in by her or subsequently acquired in the course of the marriage—are estimated, and the husband has to cover any deficiency in the total; he will also have to repay the cash he had received. It is desired to ensure that on the dissolution of the marriage the wife shall leave with belongings equal in value to those she brought in.[1]

So far we have distinguished between divorce initiated by the husband and divorce initiated by the wife, and we have discussed the different financial consequences of each. This distinction, however, is not sufficient; if there were no additional provisions, there would be automatic penalization of the party initiating divorce, in disregard of the obvious possibility that the other party, by its acts or omissions, may actually bear the blame.[2] This is a factor which must be taken into account, and we shall see that both C 15 and K 7 do so to some extent. They differ in the legal techniques employed, but it is exactly by considering them together that they can be best understood. Both set up brief lists of 'must-nots', the details of which are as follows:

1. The husband is not entitled to marry a second woman (C 15: 31 ff., K 7: 36 f.).[3] The clause refers to the taking of a second lawful wife, not to extramarital intercourse by the husband. This is clear from the use, in K 7, of the term *le'intu*—'in wifehood', as already pointed out by Kraeling.[4]

---

[1] Cf. 'Marriage Contracts', p. 19. There are express provisions to that effect in a number of demotic contracts; e.g. P. Hauswaldt 6, 219 B.C. (Lüddeckens, no. 23): (*Zu*) *dem Termin des Entlassens dich* (*als*) *Ehefrau, welches ich tun werde, oder beliebst du zu gehen selbst, gebe ich dir die Art deiner Frauensachen, die du gebracht hast in mein Haus mit dir, oder ihren Wert* (*in*) *Silber gemäß dem Preise, welcher geschrieben ist bezüglich ihrer,* . . .

[2] Cf. Levy. op. cit., p. 80.　　　　　　　[3] See 'Marriage Contracts', p. 24.

[4] Provisions forbidding the taking of a second wife are not unexpected in a polygamous society. There are contractual forerunners, possibly paving the way for monogamy imposed by law, though this process may in actual fact be a very prolonged one. The earliest clause of this kind I have found is in an Old Assyrian document, EL 1; parallels from Nuzi are text 55, in E. A. Speiser and R. H. Pfeiffer, AASOR xvi (1936), and text 25 in C. H. Gordon, 'Nuzi Tablets Relating to Women', *Analecta Orientalia*, xii (1935), pp. 171 f. A similar provision occurs in the Neo-Babylonian text Nebuchadrezzar 101, J. Kohler and F. E. Peiser,

2. The husband is not entitled to alienate his property (C 15: 35 f.). This has already been discussed.[1]

3. Rules concerning the mutual behaviour of the spouses are laid down in K 7: 37 ff., but the details are rather obscure. The husband shall be obliged (double negative: 'he shall not be able not to') to treat his wife as is customary (literally, 'do to her the law of one or two of the wives of his companions'). There are parallel provisions concerning the behaviour of the wife towards the husband. Ginsberg (p. 159) interprets the provision as referring to a refusal of intercourse.

4. A further prohibition, in K 7: 33 f., concerns the remarriage of the wife, in case of predecease of the husband. This will be considered in detail in the next chapter.[2,3]

The interesting feature emerging from a comparison of the two documents is the difference in the sanctions in the case of contravention. C 15 imposes in both the cases—1 and 2—a heavy penalty, 200 shekels, upon the husband. Prima facie this is a clumsy device, easy to evade, at the price of divorce. If the husband's heart is set, say on marrying a second wife, he can, instead of incurring the penalty, divorce his wife, at considerably lower cost to himself: return of the dowry of some 65 shekels (which include also the *mohar* of 5 shekels). This must have been obvious to the parties, and it seems therefore that the true purpose would be to compel the husband, if he is unwilling to abstain from contravening the provision, to take the initiative of divorce. The device thus achieves the result that the initiative is taken by the person to be blamed.

In K 7 the apodosis embodying the sanction in case of contravention consists of two parts: a definition, 'divorce it is' (*śin'ah hi*), and an operative direction, 'he shall do to her the law of divorce'.[4] One might have wished that the formulation were clearer; at one stage, putting the stress on the definition, I was

---

Aus dem babylonischen Rechtsleben I, 1890, p. 7. Cf. also Genesis 31. 50, where Jacob is prohibited (by treaty) from taking further wives.

[1] See p. 52, above.   [2] See pp. 73 f., below.

[3] Comparable lists of prohibitions occur in some early Greco-Egyptian marriage contracts: P. Elephantine 1, P. Giessen 2, P. Genève 21, P. Tebtunis 104.

[4] Cf. the discussion of the 'diagnosis-pattern', pp. 110 ff., below.

led to believe that the act of contravention itself counts as an act of divorce, hence 'divorce by conduct'.[1] But probably the interpretation of the provision as a whole ought to start from the fact that it replaces the penal stipulation of 200 shekels, in C 15. These 200 shekels, we suggested, have the purpose of compelling the party to be blamed to take the initiative in divorce. Under K 7, therefore, if the husband, for example, enters upon a bigamous marriage, 'divorce it is; he shall do to her the law of divorce', must mean that the aggrieved wife will be able to demand, in reliance on the marriage contract, that the husband divorce her. Formally the initiative in the act of divorce itself will be the husband's and the consequent financial disadvantages will fall on him.

The technique employed in K 7 is no doubt the more advanced one. It dispenses with a possibly ineffective penalty clause, and its usefulness is illustrated also by the clause concerning the remarriage of the widowed Yehoyishma. Instead of going into details of her duty to return the property of Anani b. Ḥaggai to his family, the document simply states that this act 'is divorce'. The equation of the remarriage of a widow with divorce from her first husband is a considerable feat of legal abstraction.

Two of the documents rule on the manner of repayment: in C 15 and K 7 the immediacy of the wife's right to the return of her belongings is stressed, in the former in the case of divorce by the husband, in the latter without distinction as to which of them initiates the divorce. The return of her property precedes her departure from the matrimonial home, and it is to take place *beyom ḥad bekhaf ḥadah*—'on one day, at one time'. A return in instalments, such as occurs, for example, in Roman sources (Ulpianus 6. 8), is thus precluded. In some demotic documents the husband is allowed 30 days for repayment of the dowry.[2] Greco-Egyptian marriage contracts envisage immediate ($\pi\alpha\rho\alpha$-

---

[1] See p. 53, note 3, above.

[2] e.g. P. Louvre 2429, of 232 B.C.? (Lüddeckens no. 15): if the dowry is not returned within 30 days, a penalty of 5 deben becomes due. See also P. British Museum 10607, of 186 B.C. (Lüddeckens no. 30); P. British Museum 10609, of 190–186 B.C. (Lüddeckens no. 31).

χρῆμα) return by the divorcing husband, but permit some delay when the wife takes the initiative.[1]

There might be need for special rules or arrangements in case as a result of the husband's activities the property of the wife increased in value. We find such provisions in C 9, the supplement of C 8, in which latter the father of Mivṭaḥiah gives her a building-plot, probably on the occasion of her marriage with Jezaniah b. Uriah. C 9 defines the position of the husband with regard to the property. He is to develop it and in return he is to have the use of it, but he is expressly denied the power of alienation. In case the couple separate, the husband is to retain the use of all or half, according to the circumstances, and in due course the property is to revert to their children.[2]

Divorce at Elephantine is not, *per se*, to be construed as a judicial act. But differences of opinion between the separating spouses with regard to their property rights, in general, or with regard to ownership of certain chattels, in particular, may have necessitated recourse to the court. A rule making return of the dowry depend, if the husband so demanded, on the wife taking an oath, is suggested by a series of demotic marriage contracts, in which the husband expressly renounces this power.[3] It is such a rule which probably underlies the deed of 'removal' C 14 executed, after divorce, by the husband, who declares himself satisfied with the oath taken by his divorcee. The variety of chattels listed in C 14[4] makes it unlikely that the proceedings decided by the oath and terminated by the document were of the nature of an ordinary litigation concerning ownership.

Little need be said about the departure from the matrimonial home. The dissolution of the marriage inevitably involves also

---

[1] e.g. 10 days' delay is granted in P. Tebtunis 104 (92 B.C.), 30 days in P. Rylands 154 (A.D. 66).

[2] The details are uncertain; cf. Cowley, pp. 28 f.

[3] The earliest of these documents is P. Hauswaldt 4 (247–221 B.C.). After listing the chattels brought in by the wife, the husband declares as follows: *Nicht soll ich können geben einen Eid hinter dich wegen deiner Frauensachen, welche oben geschrieben sind, sagend: 'Nicht hast du sie gebracht in mein Haus mit dir.'* Cf. also Lüddeckens, pp. 286 f.; for comparable Talmudic arrangements, see Mishnah Kethuboth 9. 5, and Rabinowitz, p. 39.   [4] See p. 32, above.

the spatial separation of the spouses, their going apart.[1] In patrilocal marriage, which seems to have been the rule in Elephantine, it is always the wife who leaves: on marriage she had come to the house of the husband, now she has to return to the house of her father (K 7: 28), or she may go whither she will (C 15: 25, 29; K 7: 24). The freedom of movement (*Freizügigkeit*) conceded to her is reminiscent of provisions in demotic, Greco-Egyptian and Talmudic bills of divorce, expressly empowering the wife to enter upon a second marriage.[2]

---

[1] See Levy, op. cit., pp. 77 ff.

[2] See P. Berlin 3076 (513 B.C.), 3077 (488 B.C.): *Mache dir einen Gatten*; P. Berlin 3079 (489 B.C.): *Mache dir einen Gatten an irgendeinem Orte, wohin du gehen wirst*. Later the clause becomes much more detailed; see, for example, P. Philadelphia University Museum, of 282 B.C. (J. N. Reich, *Mizraim*, i (1933), pp. 138 f.): 'I have abandoned thee as wife. I am removed from thee regarding the "law of wife". It is I who has said unto thee: "Make for thyself a husband". I shall not be able to stand before thee in any place where thou goest to make for thyself a husband there.'

For Greco-Egyptian provisions see, for example, *Berliner griechische Urkunden*, no. 1103 (13 B.C.) and P. Grenfell ii. 76 (A.D. 305–6). Of Jewish sources, cf. Mishnah Giṭṭin 9. 3 and P. Murabba'at 19.

VI

Succession

No Elephantine text deals expressly with the rules of intestate succession.[1] But some general principles can be deduced from the documents, for instance, from contractual provisions which envisage the passing of rights and duties as a consequence of the death of their bearer. What we must have in mind at the moment is such passing as is actually independent of the document, even though expressly referred to. We shall see, however, that possibly in some cases the document, the contract, itself determines the passing on death.

The transfer of rights ('active succession') is envisaged by the phrase 'and thy sons after thee' (*uvenakh 'aharakh*), usual in conveyances, in the clauses defining the rights of the alienee. The children are 'to have power' over the property after the alienee, or 'it is to be theirs' after him.[2] It is possible that at some early stage, in the absence of such a phrase, the property would not have passed to the son. In the Elephantine documents it still stresses that the conveyance is not limited to the lifetime of the present alienee, but probably was no longer essential. It is this survival of rights after the death of their bearer, in other words their capability of being inherited, which is one of the main distinctions between ownership and usufruct. The phrase must not be understood as in any way limiting the power of the alienee to transfer his right to a third person. Where such a limitation is intended other formulations are used. Two documents containing such restrictive provisions are C 9, K 4.[3]

We also find that the promises of non-interference usually given in the conveyances are, as a rule, extended so as to safe-

---

[1] The term 'intestate' is convenient, even if not quite exact, since it implies the existence of succession according to testament. It is not suggested that that was known at Elephantine.

[2] See p. 83, below.   [3] See 'Conveyances', p. 258.

guard also the children of the alienee, his brothers &c., in other words his successors in title (yet no such general term is employed; it is preferred to give detailed lists, of varying length). Penal stipulations are extended correspondingly, for example, C 20: 10 ff.: 'We shall not be able . . . to sue you . . . or to sue your sons and brothers and anyone of yours . . . and if we . . . do sue you or sue your sons or daughters or man of yours,— whoever sues will give unto you, or your sons or whomever they sue, a penalty of silver, 10 karsh. . . .'

As for the passive side, the passing of duties, we have seen that the sons of a debtor are bound to pay his debts. We have also seen that *potestas* is inadequate to explain these provisions,[1] hence we must assume that they follow from the ordinary rules of succession. The duty cannot simply be a creation of the contract, since this would imply imposing a burden upon a person not party to it (nor always under the authority of the debtor[2]), and this is not plausible. On the other hand, we do not know whether, for the creditor to be able to claim from the heirs, a special term to this effect is required.[3] Nor indeed do we know whether heirs are bound to accept the inheritance or are entitled to reject it, and—in this connexion—whether their liability is limited to the value of the assets which have actually come down to them. C 20 mentions an action brought by the heirs of a depositor against the sons of the depositee, but this is quite inconclusive as regards the more general question.

Just as penal stipulations operate in favour of the successors of the promissee, it is only to be expected that they should bind the successors of the promisor. A different solution would be impracticable, since the security of tenure which it is desired to ensure by the promise of a penalty would depend upon the accident of the promisor's survival, whereas his successors would be free to disregard his undertakings.

There is only one document, C 28, which is directly concerned with (intestate?) succession. It is less instructive than one might have hoped. Two sons of Mivṭaḥiah, Yedoniah and Maḥseiah,

[1] See p. 41, above.   [2] See p. 41, above.
[3] Cf. Seidl, *Rechtsgeschichte*, p. 69.

divide their mother's slaves between them; each takes one slave, whereas the assignment of a slave-woman and her child is deferred. To all appearances the two heirs share equally. But as we do not know whether either of them was a first-born son, no light is shed by the document on the question of a possible preferential right of a first-born. After declaring that the two brothers have reached agreement concerning the division, the document is devoted to securing the rights of one of the brothers, Yedoniah, in the slave falling to him. From this fact it can be deduced with a fair degree of probability that Yedoniah, not his brother, was in possession of all the documents of Mivṭaḥiah's archive which have come down to us. We may assume that a document parallel to C 28 was executed to assure Maḥseiah's title to the other slave.

We have no direct information concerning the rights on intestacy of a daughter, but some points are implied in the conveyances. It is fairly certain that she had a claim in the absence of sons of the deceased (as laid down also in biblical law, Numbers 27. 8). So much is indicated by the inclusion of females in the lists of possible successors to the alienee's title ('active successors') as well as in the lists of successors to the alienor ('passive successors'), bound by his assurance that there will be no interference with the alienee. In these lists we find not only the daughter of the deceased, but also his sister.[1] So we may safely conclude that a daughter (or sister) is not necessarily excluded from the inheritance. Concerning the daughter, this conclusion is supported by the provisions in the marriage contracts C 15, K 7, relating to the rights of the surviving spouse in the absence of a male or *female* child (*bar dekhar *weniqvah*).

But this is the limit of our knowledge: we do not know whether a daughter or a sister of the deceased is able to compete with male successors of equal proximity, that is to say, with a son or brother, respectively, of the deceased. On the whole it seems that she is not. For one thing, we have the biblical

---

[1] The 'active' sister is mentioned in C 6 and 25. The 'passive' sister occurs in C 1, 5, 8, 13, &c.

parallel, for another there is the relatively frequent occurrence of gift in Elephantine, and it is always women who are the donees. This does suggest an inferiority in intestate succession which it was sought to overcome by resort to gifts. But once more the small number of documents available demands caution in our conclusions.

'Mother and father' occur once in such a list of possible successors, in K 4. Even without this evidence (which is isolated and therefore not conclusive) it would on general grounds be reasonable to assume that, in the absence of descendants, the father of the deceased would have a claim to his inheritance. In biblical law the father is indeed not mentioned among the heirs, a fact which gave rise to speculation already in ancient times.[1] The explanation is simple: the provisions of Numbers 27. 8–11 concern the devolution of the family estate, which could not be owned by a son before the death of his father;[2] they do not imply a generally negative attitude to succession by the father. Whether or not the father would have precedence over the brother (or sister) of the deceased, we cannot know for certain, but it is by no means impossible.[3] When one turns to the mother, the situation is rather more complicated. There is no evidence for any right of hers under Babylonian or biblical law; such a right might have involved the transfer of property from the family of the father to that of the mother, and this was not considered desirable.[4] In Egyptian documents the mother occurs in lists of parties together with the father, and these Egyptian lists are the source on which K 4 probably draws; beyond this nothing is known of any right of the mother. Under Talmudic law she is expressly excluded from the inheritance.[5] In Roman law it was only under the senatusconsultum Tertullianum, of the

---

[1] See Philo, *De Vita Mosis*, 2. 244–5, *De Legibus Specialibus*, 2. 129–32.

[2] S. E. Loewenstamm, *Kirjath Sepher*, xxxiv (1958–9), p. 47.

[3] In K 4 the father and the mother precede brother and sister in the list. This might perhaps be taken as indicating superior rights, but, again, too much reliance cannot be put on a single document. In Talmudic law the father inherits from his deceased son and excludes his other sons, the brothers of the deceased. Philo (ibid.) carefully evades this particular point.

[4] Cf., *mutatis mutandis*, Numbers 36. 1–12; Driver and Miles, p. 337.

[5] Mishnah Baba Bathra 8. 1. See, however, the minority view at Babylonian Talmud, Baba Bathra 114b.

time of Hadrian, that the mother, in certain circumstances, became heir to the property of her deceased child.[1]

As to the claims of the widower or the widow on the estate of the deceased spouse, we must turn again to the marriage contracts. We shall take C 15 as our starting point, and discuss later the peculiarities of K 2 and 7. In C 15: 17 ff. it is provided that if the husband, Ashor, should die without having a male or female child from Mivṭaḥiah, she is to have power (*šalliṭah*) over all his property ('his goods and his chattels and all that he has on the face of all the earth'). In case of Mivṭaḥiah's predecease, and in the absence of a male or female child, Ashor, her husband, is to inherit (*yerath*) her belongings.

Prima facie the provisions in C 15 (and those in K 7) depend on there being no children of the couple alive at the time of the death of the spouse. It would not, however, be safe to deduce from this that in the presence of children the widower or the widow would have no claim to the property of the deceased spouse, or to part of it. It is possible that in the normal case, where there are children, the surviving spouse had a claim under law or custom, while the exceptional case had to be taken care of by the marriage contract. It may be mentioned in analogy that the Code of Hammurabi regulates the position of the widow where there are children (sec. 172), but there is no provision in case the husband should die without children.[2] In Talmudic law the widower has precedence over the children of his deceased wife, and excludes them from the inheritance. But for the Aramaic papyri we must be content with a *non liquet*.[3]

To go by the text of the document, the corresponding provisions in K 2 are not restricted to the case where there are no children. It is possible, however, that this deviation is only apparent. At the time of the marriage there was already a son (Palṭi, mentioned in line 13 of the document), presumably the child of the bridegroom. Hence it may well have been regarded as unpropitious to mention expressly the possibility of the couple dying childless. If so, the provision, in spite of the absence of a restriction, is in fact meant for this contingency only.

[1] Cf. *Tijdschrift voor Rechtsgeschiedenis*, xxv (1957), pp. 389 ff.
[2] See Driver and Miles, p. 334. See, however, the Neo-Babylonian laws, sec. 12.
[3] See, however, p. 77, below, on the provisions of K 4.

In the absence of children it seems that the rights of the surviving husband do not derive from the marriage contract, but are laid down by the law. This, though not proven, is at least suggested by the use of the term 'to inherit' (*yerath*), in both C 15 and K 7 (as a matter of fact, it is only in the context of the rights of the widower that the verb occurs in the Elephantine documents).

Once more K 2 deviates from the pattern of the other two documents: the same term 'to have power' (*šalliṭ*) is here applied to both husband and wife. An explanation may perhaps be found in the status of the wife Tamut, who, we may recall, was a slave-girl. It is possible that, at law, her master would be entitled to all she might leave at her death. The husband's right is in this case derived from the contract, not from a provision of the law, and hence the term *verath* is not used.

This view is perhaps supported by the strange erasures in lines 11 and 12 of the document. The provisions, as they now stand, give the surviving spouse power over all that had belonged to the deceased. An examination of the erasures has, however, led me to suggest that originally the arrangement covered only half the property.[1] The explanation is probably to be sought in the desire of the master of Tamut to retain for himself (or for his son) part of her inheritance.[2] Only at the last moment, after the contract had already been written, was he prevailed upon to change his mind. Perhaps it was pointed out to him that the possible loss to Tamut might be much greater than the gain he could anticipate: very likely, the husband's property was considerably in excess of hers. Thereupon the document was brought into line with the other marriage contracts, where the bride is free.

The suggestion then is that, apart from special circumstances, such as those reflected in K 2, the husband's title to the property of his dead wife rests on a provision of law. If that is so, we ought to account for the inclusion of the clause in the contract. There are two possible explanations: in all three contracts the husband's predecease is dealt with first, and it is likely that originally only this case, where the legal regulation was inadequate, was mentioned. Later the parties or their advisers may have felt that

[1] See full details in JNES xx (1961), pp. 129 f.
[2] A comparable, even though not identical, situation obtains in sec. 176 of the Code of Hammurabi. The case considered there is a marriage between a slave and a free woman: in case of his predecease the property acquired since their marriage is to be divided between the master and the widow (taking on behalf of her children).

a contract referring only to the husband's predecease was lacking in balance, and therefore a clause about his rights in the case of the predecease of the wife was added. In other words, we would explain the clause by reference to the structure of the document and a desire for symmetry.

But maybe it should be explained by reference to substantive law: the rule that a husband (in the absence of children) inherits the belongings of his deceased wife, though in conformity with Talmudic law, yet differs from early Oriental law, which prefers the reversion of the dowry to her family.[1] Even in late Talmudic practice we find parties arrange for return of the wife's property to her family—contrary to the provisions of the law.[2] If, then, the rules at Elephantine concerning a husband's right of succession were in accordance with Jewish law,[3] but different from other Oriental systems and also from what might occur in Jewish practice (as distinguished from law), it may have seemed desirable to make express mention of his rights, in order to avoid doubts and conflicts.

The position of the childless widow is quite different from that of the widower. Her rights, if any, are in Elephantine always created by contract, and here we are leaving the sphere of intestacy and entering upon that of dispositions in contemplation of death. Since the rights of the widow are left to be determined by the marriage contract, it will not surprise that there are considerable variations from case to case. We shall deal with these; but first of all, we would again stress the interesting terminological detail that the verb *yerath*—'to inherit' is not used of the widow. In C 15, while the widower 'inherits', the widow 'has power' (*šalliṭah*). In K 7 the husband 'inherits'; the provision concerning the surviving wife is damaged, but it

---

[1] Code of Hammurabi, secs. 163, 164; Neo-Babylonian laws, sec. 10. The husband is, however, refunded the brideprice.

[2] Palestinian Talmud, Kethuboth 33a: 'R. Jose said: and those who write, "If she dies without children, her property shall revert to the house of her father",—this is a condition relating to matters of property, and the condition stands.'

[3] At any rate with Talmudic law. No rules are mentioned in the Bible. The case of the daughters of Zelophehad (Numbers 36. 3–4) may envisage the usual situation where the property would pass to the children of the wife. There is no way for establishing just how early the Talmudic rule was.

seems clear that *yerath* is not used.[1] The term *šalliṭ*—'to have power' is not exact and well defined. In conveyances 'power over a chattel' granted to the alienee probably denotes full ownership; but the term occurs also in C 9: 11, and there it is evident from the context that usufruct only is meant. In the marriage contracts the use of *šalliṭ*, by itself, cannot furnish information as to the exact nature of the arrangement. That will in each case have to be ascertained from other data, if such are available.

L. Freund has commented on the use of *yerath* for the husband and *šalliṭah* for the wife.[2] He holds that the difference of terms implies a difference of rights: only the widower becomes full owner of the property of his late wife, while the widow has merely a usufruct and on her death the estate reverts to the husband's family. This is by no means implausible. In support one might argue that the purpose of the provision in favour of the wife is to improve her position as a childless widow. In the absence of such a provision the estate would probably pass at once to the family of the deceased husband. Nevertheless it is once again impossible to arrive at definite conclusions. The difference in terminology may be accounted for by the suggestion that the rights of the husband are laid down by law, whereas those of the wife rest upon the contract; and *šalliṭ*, we have seen, is equally compatible with both usufruct and ownership. Once again then, *non liquet*.

The legal position is clearer in the corresponding provisions of K 7. Here the wife has merely a usufruct promised to her, a usufruct, moreover, limited to the time of her widowhood.[3] The following are the relevant provisions, in K 7: 28 ff.:

And i[f] Ananiah should die, and a child, male or female, there is not to him from [Yehoyi]shma his wife, Yehoyishma she has [. .] . . . over his house, and his goods, and his possessions [and all that is to him.

---

[1] Cf. 'Marriage Contracts', p. 8, note 2.
[2] *Wiener Zeitschrift für die Kunde des Morgenlandes*, xxi (1907), p. 177.
[3] The interpretation offered here constitutes a definite break with that given in 'Marriage Contracts'. My reasons are set out in 'Aramaic Marriage Contracts: Corrigenda and Addenda', JSS v (1960), pp. 66 ff.

And whoever will] rise up aga[inst Yehoyishma] to drive her out
from his house, [of Ananiah, and his goods, and his possessions], and
all that is [to him, he shall gi]ve to h[er a fi]ne of silver karsh 20
by [royal] weight, silver 2R to the 10, and he shall do [to her] the
law of this document, and no suit (shall obtain).

But Yeh[oyishma] has no power [to] marry another husband
ex[cept] Anani, and if she does thus, divorce it is, they shall do to
[her the law of divorce.

And if] [Yehoyishma] should die, and a child, [male] or female,
there is not to her from Anani her hus[band, Anani] he shall inherit
from her, her [substance], and her goods, and her possessions, and
all that is to her.

It is unfortunate that we do not know what verb or adjective
was used to define the rights of Yehoyishma in the property of
Ananiah ('she has [. .] . . . over his house . . .'). We only know
that it was neither *yerath* nor *šalliṭ*. Her hold over the property,
pro tempore, is secured by the penalty of 200 shekels imposed
upon anyone who should attempt to expel her from it. An
identical provision is indeed contained in C 15. However, there
it follows not the provisions in contemplation of death, but those
concerning divorce. To obscure matters even further, the first
word of the clause in C 15 is damaged: only an introductory
w. .—'and' remains, two letters are missing. If one bears in mind
the context of divorce, at first sight it would seem quite plausible
to restore *we[hen] yequm* . . .—'and [if] he (i.e. the husband)
will rise up, &c.' Sayce and Cowley did so already in the *editio
princeps*, and they were widely followed. When K 7 was published, the clause under discussion was found to be damaged at
the very same place, so it is not surprising that the restoration
generally accepted for C 15 should have been transferred to K 7.
But the restoration (and all that follows from it) is shown to be
wrong when one compares a demotic marriage contract of
198 B.C., also from Elephantine, P. Berlin 13593.[1] This document contains a clause, unparalleled in any other demotic
marriage contract, but identical with that under discussion.
There are for once no gaps, and the clause begins as follows:
'Jedermann in der Welt (*p3 rmt nb (n) p3 t3*) der dich aus

---

[1] Published by W. Erichsen, *Abhandlungen der Preußischen Akademie der Wissenschaften*, 1939, no. 8 (= Lüddeckens no. 28).

meinem Hause werfen wird. . . .' Applying *jedermann in der Welt*
to the Aramaic documents, we have to conclude that the correct
reading in C 15 and K 7 is not *wehen yequm*, &c., but *we[zi]
yequm* . . . —'and whoever will rise up . . .'. This minute change
greatly affects the interpretation of the clause. It is not directed
against an act of the husband, but is designed to protect the
widow from interference with her enjoyment of the property of
her deceased husband. In C 15 the clause is at the wrong place,
not among the provisions concerning the death of the husband,
but following the provision concerning divorce. This misled
Cowley to formulate his distinction between legal divorce and
'illegal expulsion' of the wife, the latter combated by the im-
position of a heavy fine.

But the widow's right in the property of her late husband is in
K 7 limited to the time of her widowhood. If she remarries, that
puts her on the same footing as a divorcee, i.e. she will be able
to keep what is her own, but the property of her deceased
husband will revert to his family. Rights limited to the time of
widowhood are known in other ancient Eastern sources,[1] as
also in Talmudic law.[2]

Are rights defeasible by remarriage capable of being inherited, if the bearer stays a widow? Such an arrangement is
not impossible, but it is rather unlikely. Substantially, it would
not improve the position of the widow, since *ex hypothesi* she
cannot alienate *inter vivos*. She would become full owner only at
the moment of her death, for the sole purpose of passing the
property on to her heirs. In the absence of evidence to the
contrary we may assume that the rights granted to Yehoyishma
under K 7 are not capable of being inherited.

We have then so far two cases: in C 15[3] the childless widow has
either usufruct (for life) or ownership, in K 7 she has usufruct
durante viduitate. There is, however, another document, this time

---

[1] See, for example, sec. 172 of the Code of Hammurabi; also the Middle-
Assyrian document KAJ 9 (P. Koschaker, *Neue keilschriftliche Rechtsurkunden aus der
El-Amarna-Zeit*, 1928, pp. 155–6).

[2] See, for example, Mishnah Kethuboth 4. 12, Tosefta Kethuboth 11. 5, 7. Cf.
also P. Murabba'at 20 (in Aramaic), 116 (in Greek).

[3] And probably also in K 2.

not a marriage contract, but a deed of 'removal', C 25, from which it can be deduced with a fair degree of probability that a widow might get full ownership in the property of her late husband. Apparently all depended on the desire of the parties as expressed in the marriage contract.

C 25 is executed to terminate litigation between a nephew of Mivṭaḥiah's first husband, and her children from her later marriage with Ashor. The following is the family-tree as far as here relevant:[1]

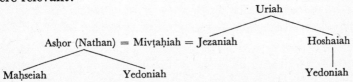

The litigation concerned the house of Jezaniah b. Uriah, who married Mivṭaḥiah in 460 B.C. It is probable that this is the house mentioned in C 8, as bordering on the plot given to Mivṭaḥiah by her father in that document.[2] We have little information about Mivṭaḥiah's (first?) marriage, that with Jezaniah. But we may assume (a) that there was no issue to the marriage, alive at the time of the death of Jezaniah. For had there been, they would have had precedence in claiming any property left by him; (b) that the marriage was terminated not by divorce but by the death of the husband. Had there been a divorce, this would have meant the end of any property relations between the parties, so that the sons of Mivṭaḥiah, not themselves in any way related to Jezaniah, would not have been able to hold on to the house, unless, indeed, he had transferred the house to her *inter vivos*, with no strings attached, which is not very likely.

The point here of immediate interest is that the rights of Mivṭaḥiah in the house of her late husband were capable of being inherited by her children from a different marriage; in other words her rights in that house must have amounted to full ownership. It is significant that her own hold over the house was not challenged; it is only after her death that a relative of her

[1] For further details cf. Cowley, p. 84.   [2] Cf. the map, Kraeling, p. 81.

late husband, the son of his brother, decided to test the rights of her sons and heirs. Evidently it is the wording of the marriage contract which is decisive as to the scope and nature of the rights of the widow. The contract must have been opened in court and examined there, which may be the reason why it is not preserved. Once it had achieved its purpose and determined the outcome of the litigation, it was for all practical purposes superseded by the abstract[1] deed of submission executed by the loser, and there would be little need to safeguard further the forty-four-year-old marriage contract.

The deed of submission is elaborated in great detail. Jezaniah's nephew renounces only his own claims, and those of any possible successors of his, but he stresses that the sons (if any?) of Jezaniah are not to be affected by the document. As the parties can hardly expect the sudden appearance of any descendants of the deceased, the addition seems to have little purpose. In any case, if descendants of the deceased Jezaniah did indeed come forth, obviously the litigation and the deed of submission C 25, being *res inter alios actae*, would not affect any claims of theirs, whether or not this claim was expressly safeguarded.

We now leave the specific question of provision for the widow, and turn to dispositions in contemplation of death generally; of these there are several instances in the Elephantine documents. Our discussion is primarily concerned with the death of the donor; some documents contain provisions concerning the devolution of the property in case of the donee's death. To these also attention will be paid.

In connexion with divorce we already referred to C 9, defining the rights of Jezaniah b. Uriah in land donated to his wife Mivṭaḥiah.[2] He is to have the use of the land, but is expressly denied the power of alienation: after the death of the couple the property is to pass to their children. We do not know whether the couple, acting in concert, would have been able to overrule the provisions of the document in favour of the children, or

---

[1] Since it does not state the factual background of the case nor the reasons for the result.   [2] See p. 63, above.

whether their children (if they had had any) would have been able to assert their rights against them.

K 4, of 434 B.C., is a deed of gift whereby Anani b. Azariah, with immediate effect (as opposed to a gift *mortis causa*) gives half a house to his wife Tamut. The deed contains provisions in contemplation of death of both the donee (the wife) and the donor (the husband). After the death of the donee[1] the gift is to pass to their children; after the death of the donor[1] they are to receive also the part of the house not included in the gift. Two children are mentioned, a son called Palṭi, and their daughter Yehoyishma. Prima facie, the son and the daughter are here treated equally.

The provisions of K 4 may be compared with those of the marriage contract K 2. There, it will be recalled, it is arranged that the property of a deceased spouse is to pass to the survivor. We have suggested that this may actually be meant only for the case where there are no descendants. K 4 supports this suggestion, since, while the children are to inherit on the death of either parent, there is no provision in favour of a surviving spouse.

The children are not a party to the agreement, although the son, Palṭi, is at its time at least fifteen years old.[2] It is of interest that the contractual arrangements between the husband and the wife, by which the children are to be beneficiaries, apparently give no direct rights to the latter. In K 12, executed thirty-two years after K 4, the donor and the donee join in selling the house to their son-in-law, the husband of Yehoyishma. Of the children mentioned in K 4, at least Yehoyishma seems to have been alive at the time of K 12, yet there is no reference to any right of hers, arising out of the former document. However, though it seems clear that the donor and the donee, acting in agreement, are able to disregard the provisions in favour of a third party contained in the document, it is possible that the donee alone would be unable to do so.

[1] 'At the age of 100 (?) years.' The reading of the numeral is not quite certain. If it is correct, then the optimal age of K 4 is reminiscent of Isaiah 65. 20, and also of some Neo-Assyrian letters. See L. Waterman, *Royal Correspondence of the Assyrian Empire*, 1930, Letters 113, 114, 115, 427, 494.

[2] K 4 is of 434 B.C.; Palṭi was first mentioned in K 2, of 449 B.C.

The phrase *beḥayyay uvemothi*—'in my life and at my death',
occurs in two Elephantine documents, C 8: 3, 8; K 10: 11, 13.
Both are cases of gift with immediate effect. The phrase has
nothing to do with dispositions in contemplation of death; its
purpose is rather to stress that a certain state of affairs is *not* to be
affected by the death of the donor.[1] It contrasts with *bemothi*—
'at my death', of K 5: 4, 9: 17, 18, which is designed to defer the
effect of the transaction till the death of the manumitter or
donor, respectively.

We have already considered in detail K 5, the deed of manumission of Tamut and Yehoyishma. It is made in contemplation
of the manumitter's death and is to take effect only at that
moment. Line 3 ff.: 'I have taken thought for thee in my life,
free have I relinquished thee (with effect) at my death, and I
have relinquished Yehoyishma by name, thy daughter, whom
thou didst bear me.'[2]

K 9, of 404 B.C., is a gift in contemplation of death, to come
into force at the donor's death. Anani gives Yehoyishma part of
a house 'at my death in affection, because she did maintain me
when I was old in days and was not able (to work) with my
hands, and she did maintain me. Moreover I give it to her at
my death' (lines 17 ff.). In line 21 f. the donor declares the gift
to be irrevocable. No one shall be able 'to bring forth against
thee a document, new or old, but this document which I made
out to thee is valid (*meyaṣṣav*)'.[3]

Both K 5 and 9 contain the interesting phrase *'anah 'asteth
lekhi beḥayyay*—'I have taken thought for thee in my life', which
clearly marks the transaction as one made in contemplation of
death, as then expressed also by *bemothi*—'at my death'. The
peculiar wording of the phrase is an idiom playing upon the
contrast of life and death, and no legal import should be
attached to it.

---

[1] For a detailed comparative discussion of the phrase, see *Gifts*, pp. 120 ff.
[2] See pp. 38 f., above.   [3] See Kutscher, p. 237.

VII

The Law of Property

OUR material for the law of property is relatively ample. More than half of the Elephantine documents are concerned with property rights. These are deeds of 'conveyance', in the wide sense in which we here use this term.[1] In spite of the obvious differences between, for example, a deed of gift and a deed of 'removal', there remains the basic similarity both in substance—transfer or recognition of rights—and in the schemata of the documents. We are therefore justified in considering them together.

We have already dealt with deeds of submission (or 're-moval').[2] Deeds of gift are frequent among our documents. This is interesting since it leads to doubt, for Aramaic Elephantine at least, the validity of the principle of *notwendige Entgeltlichkeit* ('need for consideration'),[3] stressed by Seidl for Egyptian law.[4] All the donees are women, and we have already pointed to the possible significance of this fact with regard to the rules of in-testate succession.

Deeds of sale differ from deeds of gift in that they usually (though not always) contain also warranties given by the seller in the event of eviction of the buyer.

Conveyances are always drawn up *ex latere alienatoris*: it is the alienor who addresses the alienee. The operative part of the document of conveyance begins with a more or less brief intro-duction, setting out the facts of the transaction, and thereby disclosing its purpose and nature. Since the introduction is primarily concerned with facts, there is little occasion for stereo-typed phrases, and it may vary considerably from document to

---

[1] See pp. 3 f., above, for a classification of the various types of documents included under this heading.   [2] See pp. 33 ff., above.   [3] See p. 30, above.
[4] *Rechtsgeschichte*, pp. 40 ff.; but cf. the remarks of H. J. Wolff, *Zeitschrift der Savigny-Stiftung für Rechtsgeschichte, Romanistische Abteilung*, lxxiv (1957), pp. 413 f.

document.[1] Having read this part, one has an outline of the facts, and an idea of the document as a whole.

In the documents dealing with land, the introduction is followed by a description of the property conveyed, either (*a*) by measurements and boundaries, or (*b*) by boundaries only. In all the documents which have both measurements and boundaries, the measurements are given first, in the sequence length—width. There is no fixed order in which the boundaries are listed, but about half the documents have the sequence 'above (= north)–below (= south)–east–west'.[2] The boundaries always take the property conveyed as the centre (e.g. 'east of it is . . ., west of it is . . .,' &c.). Some documents give further details concerning the state of the property conveyed.

All this concerns land. Where moveables are transferred, the need for an elaborate description will rarely arise. It arises, for example, in C 28, where an exact description of the slaves divided among the heirs of Mivṭaḥiah is given.

Next follow the clauses which throw most light on the rules and concepts concerning property which prevailed at Elephantine, namely, the declarations of the transferor about the transfer and the legal position of the transferee.

In deeds of sale, gift, or barter, there is the statement that the transferor has 'given' (*yehav*) or 'sold and given' (*zabben wihav*) the object to the transferee. When the transferor says *yahaveth*— 'I have given' this ought to be understood in a technical sense (in other contexts the verb is non-technical). It refers not so much to the physical act of giving, as to the transfer of ownership to the alienee.[3] The nature of the giving is sometimes further defined. C 13 : 3 stresses that a former giving was *bidemohi*—'for its price'. Deeds of gift usually state that the giving is *beraḥamin*, literally 'in affection'.[4] When a donor says that he gives *beḥayyay*

---

[1] For examples, see 'Conveyances', p. 251.

[2] See Kraeling, pp. 77 ff., for the meaning of 'above' and 'below'.

[3] See already Kraeling, p. 172. Latin *dare* sometimes has this pregnant meaning of 'to transfer ownership'. See H. G. Heumann and E. Seckel, *Handlexikon zu den Quellen des römischen Rechts*, 1907, s.v.

[4] The word has also the wider, secondary meaning 'gratis', 'without consideration'. A similar semantic development underlies Hebrew *ḥinnam* and Latin *gratis*, derived from *ḥen* and *gratia*, respectively.

uvemothi—'in my life and at my death',[1] this implies two things: that the gift takes effect immediately, and that it is to be perpetual, not to be affected by the death of the donor. *Bemothi*—'at my death',[2] standing by itself, contrasts with the part '... in my life' of the former phrase: it is a giving *mortis causa*, with its effect delayed until after the death of the donor.

Sometimes the transferor declares his satisfaction—literally, 'thou hast satisfied my heart' (*hoṭevth levavi*), or 'my heart is satisfied' (*ṭiv levavi*)—with something he has received from the other party. This may be money, in deeds of sale,[3] or some act, such as an oath taken by the other party in the course of litigation.

Another term frequently occurring is *reḥaq*—'to remove (oneself)',[4] which may mean physical or legal removal, or usually a mixture of both. There are two main variants. The one (*a*) expresses the idea of separation of the parties. Normally the party with a potential claim would say *raḥqeth minnakh*—'I have removed from thee'.[5] In C 14: 11, 28: 11, the person executing the document declares himself removed from litigation, i.e. unable to litigate. In C 6: 15 the party in whose favour the document is executed is assured that he 'is removed from any litigation concerning that land'. The other variant (*b*) expresses the idea of a man withdrawing from a piece of property: the person executing the document declares himself removed from the object of the transaction.[6] As a further possibility we may mention the occurrence together of (*a*) and (*b*), in the introduction of C 25: 'I have removed from you from the house of Jezaniah.'

The notions underlying the two variants are quite different. The former (*a*) derives from procedure. Apparently in ancient

[1] C 8: 3, 8; K 10: 11, 13. See p. 78, above.
[2] K 9: 17, 18; cf. K 5: 4.
[3] Also, in marriage contracts, the brideprice (C 15: 5, K 7: 5), or the dowry (C 15: 15).
[4] 'To renounce', 'submit', would be possible renderings, but would not fit in all the texts. 'Remove', 'removal' are clumsy English, but they convey fairly exactly the meaning of the Aramaic word.
[5] See C 14: 6, 20: 9, 43: 4, 67: fragment 5; cf. also K 1: 7.
[6] C 13: 7, 16; K 3: 11, 13.

times litigation, similar to combat,[1] is thought of as 'a coming near', 'an approaching', 'a standing up against . . .'; the cession of litigation is 'a separation', 'a parting'. The latter usage (*b*) is substantive, probably expressive of the fact that in the convey-ance of land what actually happens is that the transferor abandons the land, 'removes himself' from it. Which of the two notions is the original one we cannot be sure. On the whole I would give preference to the procedural one, since it is in con-formity with the terminology concerning litigation, which, as just pointed out, is based on combat. The substantive formula-tion is, to my knowledge, without exact parallel in earlier sources.[2]

The notion of 'removal' is especially well suited for deeds of submission, and occurs in three of them, C 14, 20, 25. It is present also in the technical name *sefar mirḥaq*—'deed of removal', which, when executed after litigation by the losing party, we have occasionally rendered 'deed of submission'.[3]

The expressions so far discussed refer in form to the acts or the position of the transferor. He has given, his heart is satisfied, he has removed himself (or is removed).[4] Other expressions instead refer to the position of the transferee, the transferor recognizing his rights. In some documents the declarations of transfer are followed by one that the property is the transferee's: 'Thine it is.'[5] Sometimes, instead of 'thine it is', or in addition to it, we find the expression 'thou hast power (*šalliṭ*) over it'.[6] The scope of this 'power' is not exactly defined, and need not in all cases be the same.[7]

In many of the conveyances one of the expressions denoting transfer or recognition is followed by the phrase 'from this day and for ever'. We have already pointed out, in connexion with

---

[1] See Kutscher, p. 238.

[2] Different, yet comparable, is the use of *elû*—'to rise from (and leave)' in cunei-form documents. See 'Conveyances', p. 384, and CAD iv, pp. 124 f.

[3] See pp. 33 f., above.

[4] A freak exception in C 6: 15: the other party 'is removed from litigation'.

[5] See, for example, C 13: 7, 16; 25: 8; K 9: 11, and cf., for declarations 'acknow-ledging' the existence of a certain legal situation, p. 46, above.

[6] e.g. C 8: 9, 28: 6, K 3: 11, &c.

[7] See p. 72, above.

the marriage contracts, that this does not imply that a given legal situation is not susceptible of change, such as subsequent alienation by the present alienee. It merely denotes that the legal situation evidenced by the document is not *a priori* limited in time.

Most of the documents concerning land (and also C 28, concerning slaves) contain the provision that the children of the alienee are to succeed to his position. They are to have power over the property after him,[1] or it is to be theirs after him.[2] The import of this provision has already been discussed.[3]

In six documents[4] there is a reference to the alienee's power to transfer his rights to a third person. 'To whom thou desirest thou wilt give it.' Two of the documents are more circumstantial and mention that the alienee may transfer his rights by way of gift or by way of sale.[5]

All the deeds of sale concerning land (C 13, K 3, 12) contain this reference to the alienee's power of subsequent alienation. For the case of gift we have only the doubtful evidence of C 8; are we to infer from the silence of the other deeds of gift that there is in this respect a substantial difference between the position of a donee and that of a buyer? Again, as we have seen, in all our deeds of gift the donees are women; is this of any relevance? That is to say, would a male donee have usually been given wider rights? The material at our disposal does not warrant an answer.

Some of these phrases, in combination, constitute, in a given document, the clause setting out the legal import of the transaction. This clause will sometimes be quite short (e.g. in C 1, K 1), sometimes of considerable length (e.g. K 9).[6]

In the main, the clause concerning the legal import refers to events which have taken place prior to the execution of the document. It relates, in the perfect tense, the payment of the price, the transfer of the property, or the self-removal of the transferor from it. When describing the rights of the alienee the

[1] e.g. C 8: 9, 28: 7, K 3: 12, &c.
[2] C 13: 7, 25: 9.
[3] See p. 65, above.
[4] C 8, 13, 25, 28, K 3, 12; cf. p. 124, below.
[5] C 25, K 12.
[6] For detailed examples, see 'Conveyances', pp. 259 ff.

documents quite naturally use the present (implied in the declaration 'it [is] thine'),[1] or the imperfect ('thou wilt give', 'thou wilt sell'), or the imperative ('do so and so'—C 9). The clause refers either to acts which have been performed in the past, or to situations beginning with the completion of the transaction, but continuing to have effect also in the future (such as the ownership of the alienee and his power to alienate).

In addition the documents contain obligations incidental to the conveyance, undertaken by the alienor. These are of two kinds. First, there is in all the documents the promise that the alienor and his successors will not interfere with the alienee's enjoyment of the property. The other provision, occurring only in two of the deeds of sale (K 1, 3),[2] is a defension clause, wherein the alienor undertakes to come to the defence of the alienee should his title be contested by a third party.

The provision concerning non-interference by the alienor can be divided into three component parts: (a) A promise that there will be no challenge of the rights of the alienee. (b) If there is such a challenge, a penalty will be paid to the alienee. And (c) the property will be 'again' (*'appam)[3] that of the alienee. This tripartite promise of 'non-interference' is essentially simple and would probably be fairly uniform in all the documents, were it not for a complicating factor: usually the scribe is not content to lay down rights and duties inter partes, but considers it desirable to mention also certain other possible parties to a future dispute, viz. successors to the alienee ('active successors') and successors to the alienor ('passive successors').[4] In other words, provision is made for possible interference by the alienor and his successors against the alienee and his successors. This multiplicity of parties gives occasion for a number of variations, both with regard to the structure of the clause as a whole, and the enumeration of possible litigants. As for the structure of the clause, one may distinguish between 'simple' and 'double' clauses. A clause is 'simple', if in (a) the promise of no-challenge, it lists all the

---

[1] The term 'present' must be taken cum grano salis: there is no exact Aramaic equivalent. [2] And also in the deed of lease, P. Meissner.
[3] See p. 88, below. [4] See pp. 65 ff., above.

possible parties (as far as at all given in the particular document), and this is followed by one penalty-clause (*b*), and by one *'*appam-clause (*c*), confirming that the property will be 'again' the alienee's. A clause is 'double', if there are two separate and complete sequences (*a*), (*b*), and (*c*), the first dealing with challenge by the alienor himself, the penalty for this challenge, and the 'again' provision, the second repeating all this in respect of interference by other persons. For all the intricate variations caused by the multiplicity of parties and the different clauses we can refer to 'Conveyances', pp. 261 ff. Here it will suffice to quote one example of each type of clause:

C 6: 12 ff. (simple clause): I shall not be able to start against thee suit or process, I and my son and my daughter, brother and sister of mine, one near by and one far away,[1] concerning that land, (against) thee and thy son and thy daughter, brother and sister of thine, one near by and one far away. Whoever sues thee in my name concerning that land, shall give to thee silver, 20 karsh, royal weight, silver 2R to the ten, and the land is again thine, and thou art removed from any suit brought against thee with regard to that land.

K 3: 12 ff. (double clause): We shall not be able to start against thee suit or process concerning this house which we have sold and given (over) to thee, and from which we have removed. And we shall not be able to sue son of thine and daughter, and whomsoever thou desirest to give it to. If we start against thee suit or process and sue son and daughter of thine, and whomever thou desirest to give it to, we shall give thee silver, 20 karsh, silver 2R to the ten, and the house is thine again, and thy children's after thee, and his to whom thou desirest to give it.

And son and daughter of ours shall not be able to start against thee suit or process concerning this house, the boundaries of which are written above. If they sue thee, and sue son and daughter of thine, they shall give thee silver, 20 karsh, silver 2R to the 10, and the house is thine again, and thy children's after thee.

The simple clause looks the more modern of the two types. Presumably, at an early stage the promise was restricted to the alienor himself. Next other possible challengers were added in a separate clause. Finally the clauses were merged. In K 4, however, the doubling of the clause has a function: it is used to stipulate different penalties for interference by the alienor himself (5 karsh) and others (20 karsh).

[1] See 'Conveyances', p. 265.

As may be seen, the promise that there will be no challenge is expressed by saying that no one will be 'able', that is to say entitled,[1] to interfere with the alienee. This formulation is used in all documents, with the sole exception of C 8, which instead speaks of no one but the donee 'having power' over the land conveyed.[2] The lists of active and passive parties, sometimes very involved, are discussed in detail in 'Conveyances', pp. 264 ff., to which we refer.

What are the contents of the promise which we have called promise of 'no-challenge', or 'non-interference'? Usually that no legal steps will be taken by the alienor or others against the alienee. The usual expressions are that no one will be able 'to start suit (or process)', *rešah din (udevav)* or *gari din (udevav)*. Some documents have also *qeval 'al X (qodam) segan wedayyan*— 'to complain against X (before) prefect or judge', but it is doubtful whether this adds in any way to the substance of the provision.[3]

Penal stipulations feature prominently in the Aramaic documents. In the absence of promissory oaths,[4] they are the main safeguard ensuring the faithful discharge of undertakings; hence, undertakings not accompanied by penal pecuniary provisions are rare. This is so not only in the deeds of conveyance, but also, we have seen, in manumission,[5] adoption,[6] and marriage;[7] we shall find penal provisions also in the contracts of loan,[8] though both the formulation and the function are somewhat different. The penalties are often quite heavy, whether measured by the general level of financial dealings as evidenced in deeds of loan, sale and marriage, or by the value of the object with which the particular document is concerned. The sum is usually 5 karsh (= 50 shekels), or a multiple of it; there are only two documents, C 43, K 11, in which the penalty promised is less, 2 karsh and 1 karsh, respectively. The others range from 5 karsh[9] to

---

[1] See P. Joüon, *Mélanges de l'Université Saint-Joseph*, xviii (1934), p. 45.
[2] See 'Conveyances', pp. 264, 389.
[3] See p. 27, above, and 'Conveyances', pp. 266 f.   [4] See p. 32, above.
[5] K 5, see pp. 38 f., above.   [6] K 8, see p. 40, above.
[7] C 15, K 7; see pp. 52, 61 f., above.   [8] See p. 96, below.
[9] C 1, 5, 14, K 1, 2, 4.

10,[1] 20,[2] and 30.[3] In K 5 the stiff penalty of 50 karsh is imposed not only upon the attempt to re-enslave the two women manumitted therein, but also upon their refusal to honour their παραμονή undertakings. Finally, if the reading is correct, a penalty of 100 karsh is imposed in C 2, apparently relating to the supply of corn to the garrison at Elephantine. The document is too fragmentary to enable us to understand the reason for such a singularly heavy penalty.

There is no necessary relationship between the value of the transaction and the penalty stipulated. This can be deduced from several documents in which the value of the subject-matter is given. In C 13 a house is conveyed in exchange for property estimated at 5 karsh. The penalty stipulated is 10 karsh, the double; but this is the only case in which this ratio exists, and it must not be generalized in the face of the other documents. In C 43, a transaction concerning 6 shekels is secured by a penalty of 2 karsh. K 1 mentions a payment of 5 shekels and a tenfold penalty of 5 karsh; but it is better to disregard this document which may be the result of a compromise settlement, and perhaps does not reveal the true value of the object conveyed. Quite conclusive, on the other hand, are the deeds of sale K 3 and 12. The prices paid are 1 karsh 4 shekels and 1 karsh 3 shekels, respectively; the penalty is in each case 20 karsh. We can then sum up: penalties are on the whole independent in their amount of the value of the transaction they serve to protect,[4] and usually consist of very considerable round sums.

We have no instance of a claim for the payment of a penalty, but then we must remember that the material referring to actual litigation is very limited. At any rate, there is nothing to justify doubts as to the full legal efficacy of the penal stipulations.[5] The

---

[1] C 8, 9, 13, 20, 25, 28, K 4, 6.

[2] C 6, K 3, 4, 12; also in the marriage contracts C 15 and K 7.

[3] K 9, 10, and also in the deed of adoption K 8.

[4] In Neo-Assyrian and Neo-Babylonian documents, the penalty most commonly amounts to a fixed multiple of the sum involved, in the former to tenfold, in the latter to twelvefold.

[5] So also L. Blau, *Monatsschrift für Geschichte und Wissenschaft des Judentums*, lxiii (1919), pp. 151 f.; see, however, the remarks on some of the penal provisions of C 15, p. 61, above.

risk of having to pay a considerable sum must have caused people to abide by their obligations, and especially must have prevented an alienor from trying to go back upon the alienation.

All the penal stipulations are for the benefit of the aggrieved party. There is in the Elephantine material no instance of a stipulation in favour of a god or the king, a device to be encountered in many ancient sources, aimed at making more effective and speedier procedures available to the plaintiff.

The penal stipulation is regularly followed by a statement to the effect that the satisfactory state of affairs existing before the alienee was interfered with, will be restored.[1] The key-word in this provision is *'appam, the exact import of which, as well as its etymology, are obscure.[2] Therefore its meaning must be gathered from the legal notions of the context. Cowley rendered it by 'assuredly'; this was a mere guess and has been rightly rejected as unsatisfactory. Another suggestion is that *'appam means 'in addition', 'moreover', but there are objections to this rendering too. For one thing, one document, C 1, has a different adverb, tuv, in place of *'appam. The primary meaning of the root tuv (= Hebrew šuv) is 'to return'. For another, clauses identical with that here under discussion occur in early demotic papyri.[3] The Egyptian equivalent of *'appam is 'n, commonly rendered again, encore, wiederum.[4]

It is submitted that the correct translation of *'appam, like that of tuv in C 1 and of 'n in the demotic documents, is 'again'.[5] The idea expressed is one of return to the position which prevailed before the attack on the person acquiring rights under the document. The attack has been repelled, a penalty has been paid, and the property is again in the undisturbed possession of the alienee. The receipt of the penalty, however large, has in no way detracted from his rights. The penalty is cumulative, not alternative. We shall presently encounter this idea of return to

---

[1] For this clause, see Blau, op. cit., p. 152; Rabinowitz, pp. 48 ff.

[2] See Kraeling, p. 162.

[3] See, for example, P. Rylands 1 (643 B.C.); Cup Louvre E 706 (about 590 B.C.); and P. Louvre 10935 (553 B.C.). For a comparison of the demotic and Aramaic clauses, see Seidl, Rechtsgeschichte, p. 73.

[4] See A. Erman–H. Grapow, Wörterbuch der ägyptischen Sprache, i (1926), p. 189.

[5] And see already P. Joüon, loc. cit., pp. 29 f.

a previous state also in the defension clause, which now falls to be considered.

Only two conveyances, K 1 and 3 (and the document of lease, P. Meissner), mention an undertaking of the alienor to come to the defence of the alienee in case of claims by a third party. It might then appear that defension clauses are not in general use, but the material at our disposal does not warrant such a conclusion. Defension clauses are not to be expected where the *causa* of the conveyance is gift and the alienor has received no consideration, nor—even in sale—where the object is some moveable of little value. In fact, in our material, in addition to K 1 and 3 one might expect defension clauses only in C 13 and K 12. In both cases, however, as we have seen,[1] the alienee gets the old title-deeds, and this should afford him reasonable security, so that no need may have been felt for a further obligation of defension. With regard to K 12 we know, moreover, that the property transferred has been in the possession of the alienors for 35 years; interference by a third party is therefore not likely.

Defension clauses very similar in formulation to the Aramaic ones are common in the ancient Near East and in early demotic documents, as well as in later times. It would therefore be preferable to study them in a wide comparative setting,[2] but here we shall confine ourselves to the three documents mentioned. The obligation of the seller arises when anyone has challenged the buyer, disputing his title. The verb used for such a challenge is *gari*, usually rendered 'to start suit',[3] but the exactness of this is not beyond doubt. For the corresponding Neo-Babylonian material it has been suggested that even claims without judicial proceedings are sufficient to render the provision operative.

The clause stating the duty of the alienor contains three verbs (i) I shall stand up, (ii) I shall clean, (iii) I shall give (back) to thee. The introductory verb, 'I shall stand up', is missing in K 1. Kraeling, commenting on K 3: 20, holds that 'this is legal terminology; *qum* in effect means to take legal action'. This is possible, but not absolutely necessary. In Semitic languages verbs

---

[1] See p. 31, above.   [2] See 'Defension Clauses', pp. 15 ff.
[3] P. Meissner is damaged at this point (line 9) and restorations are uncertain.

meaning 'to stand up', or 'to go', are frequently used in an auxiliary sense, and are then best left untranslated.[1]

The core of the defension clause is the seller's undertaking 'to clean' the property sold from claims raised to it. The property is deemed contaminated by the claim, and the seller's action restores it to its former purity.[2] It is always the object which is cleaned, not the buyer. This notion of 'cleaning' (*bereinigen*) has been amply discussed, and it will suffice to refer to some of the publications.[3]

Comparison establishes beyond doubt the basic meaning 'to clean' of the verbs used in the various systems.[4] In the Aramaic documents no question arises as far as P. Meissner is concerned, which has *naqqi*—'to clean'. It is true that the two other documents, K 1 and 3, employ the verb *passel*, the etymology of which is not yet quite clear;[5] but one will hardly go wrong in assuming that here too the meaning is 'to clean', or some nuance of it.

Finally the seller promises that, having successfully defended the title, he will give (back) the chattel to the buyer. This part of the clause possibly reflects an early stage, when adjudication was not in favour of the buyer who had been challenged, but in favour of his *auctor*, the seller; it would then have been necessary to transfer the property again. At the period of the documents, however, it is probably of little importance.

Provisions in case the vendor refuses, or is unable, to fulfil his obligation to defend, are not an essential part of the defension clause; they are often missing in the clauses of ancient Eastern documents. Various provisions for the case of non-defension can

---

[1] See, however, p. 117, below.   [2] Cf. Seidl, *Rechtsgeschichte*, p. 38.

[3] See, for example, P. Koschaker, *Babylonisch-assyrisches Bürgschaftsrecht*, 1911, pp. 192 ff.; M. San Nicolò, *Die Schlußklauseln der altbabylonischen Kauf- und Tauschverträge*, 1922, pp. 170 f., 195; B. Landsberger, ZA xxxix (1930), pp. 286 ff.; Seidl, *Rechtsgeschichte*, p. 38; Rabinowitz, pp. 145 f.

[4] To mention just a few of the more important examples: in Accadian we have *ubbubu* (Susa, Kültepe), *zukku* (Nuzi, Alalakh), and *murruqu* (Neo-Babylonian); in demotic *w'b* and *n'*; in Greek καθαροποιέω (Avroman, Dura-Europos, Byzantine Egypt); in Hebrew and Aramaic *mrq* (the cognate of Neo-Babylonian *murruqu*) is the verb most frequently used (see the references, p. 118, below).

[5] Cf. Kutscher, p. 240; in 'Defension Clauses', p. 20, I have suggested a connexion with *passel*—'to peel off', of Genesis 30. 37–38.

be envisaged. There might be an undertaking to replace in kind the object of which the buyer had been deprived. Or a money-payment might be agreed upon, either identical with the price paid (possibly inclusive of improvements), or an increased sum, embodying a penal element. The two provisions might be combined: the seller undertakes to replace the object, and for the case of non-fulfilment even of this obligation a money-payment is fixed.[1] It is reasonable to assume that in such a case the payment stipulated is in excess of the value of the object which has been evicted; else the two successive obligations, replacement and money-payment, would be mere alternatives at the seller's option.

In the Aramaic papyri there are such provisions in case of non-defension in P. Meissner and K 3. In the former the provision is obscure, because of the bad state of preservation of the document. The clause in K 3 is rather elaborate: the sellers undertake 'to clean' the house within thirty days. If they have not done so by that time, they will have to give the buyer a house similar to that he has lost. Their obligation, however, is subject to a proviso: if the buyer is evicted by the children of that prior owner from whom the present sellers acquired the house, the present sellers will be able to discharge their obligation by repaying the price, plus such improvements as the buyer may in the meantime have made.[2]

We have so far dealt only with ownership, but property rights in objects owned by someone else, *iura in re aliena*, were also known in Elephantine.

First there are easements. C 5 is executed by a grantee of building rights. The document is in the main devoted to safeguarding the rights of the grantor, and it is difficult to make out the scope of the grant. Probably it is meant to be of a permanent nature, hence a real right. Rights of passage arise out of some of Anani b. Azariah's gifts to his daughter Yehoyishma. Thus in

[1] So, for example, in the demotic P. Rylands 8 (560 B.C.), M. Malinine, *Archives d'histoire du droit oriental*, v (1951), p. 56. See also the complicated and detailed arrangements in a document from Nuzi, AASOR xvi (1936), text 37.
[2] For a more detailed discussion of these involved provisions, see 'Defension Clauses', pp. 20 f.

K 6 mention is made of the right to use stairs and of a right of exit, but owing to the state of the document it is impossible to make out the details. The use of stairs and a gate is permitted in K 9: 14 ff.; cf. also K 12: 21 f.[1]

There are also cases of personal servitude, usufruct. This institution emerges fairly clearly from a number of documents. The scope of the rights of Mivṭaḥiah and Tamut, in case of widowhood, is uncertain, but the widowed Yehoyishma would have a usufruct over her husband's property as long as she did not remarry.[2] The rights of Jezaniah, Mivṭaḥiah's first husband, under C 9, can also be regarded as usufruct.

---

[1] '. . . and the gate above opens to the street of the king; from there thou shalt go forth and go in.' Cf. RIDA v (1958), p. 307.

[2] See, on the provisions of C 15, K 2 and 7, pp. 69 ff., above.

VIII

The Law of Obligations

OBLIGATIONS are but meagrely represented in the Aramaic papyri. As regards contract we have some documents of loan,[1] one contract of lease, P. Meissner, and an obscure reference to deposit, in C 20. Delictal situations may be reflected in C 7 and 45, possibly also in C 16. All the three documents are too poorly preserved to be of much use.

I. *Loan*

Two of the documents, C 10, 11, concern loans of money, the third, K 11, concerns a loan of grain. These three are true loans: the lender transfers to the borrower fungible property, to be repaid at a later date. Two fragments, C 29, 35, refer to money debts resulting from other transactions. In C 29 a debt of 1 karsh 4 shekels, part of the purchase price of a house, is acknowledged. In C 35 a man acknowledges that he owes the other party, a woman, the sum of 2 shekels, part of what was due to her under her marriage contract. Hence we may assume that the document was written after the marriage of the parties was dissolved. The difference between a loan proper and another debt is reflected in the wording of the documents. The true loan starts by stating, 'thou hast given me as a loan', hence the obligation of repayment. Such a statement would not be quite exact in the other documents, therefore a more abstract formulation is used: 'thou hast upon me' (= 'thou hast a claim against me'), a phrase which has close parallels in Accadian and demotic.[2] Though C 29 and C 35 do reveal the underlying *causa* (purchase of a house, in the one case, dissolution of marriage, in the other), presumably this could be omitted, when the docu-

---

[1] C 10, 11, K 11, and the fragmentary C 29, 35, 49.
[2] See Kutscher, p. 242; Seidl, *Rechtsgeschichte*, p. 57.

ment would become an abstract acknowledgement of indebtedness, not revealing the factual situation motivating its execution.[1]

C 49 is obscure; it is singular in that it starts off, not with an acknowledgement of indebtedness, but rather with a statement of claim: not 'I owe thee', but 'thou owest me'. It is therefore possible that this is a fragment, not of a deed of loan, but of an action brought by the creditor for the recovery of a debt.

From the point of view of the lender, the purpose of a loan is the making of a profit, the taking of interest, and in formulating the deed he will pay attention to the way in which eventual repayment of both capital and interest is to be ensured. With regard to interest it is noteworthy that no scruples are felt about stipulating it. As has often been pointed out, the relevant biblical provisions[2] are flatly disregarded in Elephantine. There is not even recourse to one of the many subterfuges resorted to, from times immemorial and almost universally, whenever it is desired to evade a ban, or restrictions, on the taking of interest.[3]

Both C 10 and 11 are loans of the rather small sum of 4 shekels, the interest on which amounts to 2 *hallurin* per shekel per month, altogether 8 *hallurin*. According to Cowley, whose conclusions seem well founded, 1 shekel contains 40 *hallurin*; hence the interest in both cases amounts to 60 per cent. per year, a rate which is very high indeed, but nevertheless bearable here because of the smallness of the amount. Probably such small loans were occasioned by some urgent personal need; they would hardly reflect business transactions of the borrower. The same holds true for K 11, a loan of spelt; as for the interest, we do not know what rate is agreed upon in this case, since the quantity lent and that to be repaid are expressed in different units, the relation between which has not yet been established; there is also some doubt concerning the numeral in line 4. Generally speaking, comparison with other sources shows that usually the interest

---

[1] See Seidl, ibid.

[2] Exodus 22. 24, Leviticus 25. 36–37, Deuteronomy 23. 20.

[3] All this applies only to C 10 and 11, where both the parties are Jewish, but not to K 11, where the lender is Gentile.

on loans of natural produce is higher than on loans of money.[1]

The papyri provide for the payment of compound interest: in C 10 and 11, interest not paid is to be added to the capital, and is itself to become interest-bearing at the same rate. As for the date of repayment, K 11 envisages it when the borrower receives his ration from the treasury, that is to say, probably within a very short period.[2] C 10 provides for distraint 'if a second year comes' before the capital and interest are fully paid, in other words, the loan is for a maximum period of one year. No date of repayment is fixed in the corresponding provision of C 11, which is not yet fully comprehensible; it is merely agreed that if the capital and the interest are not paid by a certain date,[3] they are to be 'turned' (*ya'aquf), and are to continue to bear interest until actual repayment. For *'aqaf, the basic meaning of which is 'to turn', 'to go around' (neither of which is very helpful here), Cowley suggests the translation 'be doubled'.[4] Very tentatively I would connect the provision with a rule of Egyptian law: some demotic loan-documents provide that the interest must not finally exceed *alterum tantum*.[5] Since no exact date of repayment is laid down (neither, it may be stressed, are there any provisions for distraint in this document), it may have been desired to find a way for evading the *non ultra alterum tantum* rule by 'renewing' the loan at an agreed date.[6]

We have already referred to provisions concerning evidence which are to be met in C 10 and 11.[7] The former provides that the lender's possession of the deed is conclusive proof of his not

[1] See the Laws of Eshnunna, secs. 18A, 20; Code of Hammurabi, sec. L. Cf. Driver and Miles, p. 173.

[2] For similar arrangements see *Berliner griechische Urkunden* 69 (A.D. 120) and the Latin P. Michigan vii. 438 (A.D. 140): . . . r]eddam ex stipendi[o] prox[imo . . . See V. Arangio-Ruiz, *Studi Solazzi*, 1948, p. 256.

[3] 'The month of Thoth, year 9', probably of Xerxes, 478 B.C. (cf. 'Schema', p. 43); we do not know how long after the execution of the document this is, since the beginning, containing the date, is missing.

[4] Cf. also J. Halévy, *Revue Sémitique*, xv (1907), p. 524, note 1; G. R. Driver, *Journal of the Royal Asiatic Society*, 1932, p. 72.

[5] Seidl, *Rechtsgeschichte*, p. 57. For Roman law, cf. Digesta 12. 6. 26. 1, Codex Justinianus 4. 32. 10, 4. 32. 27. 1.

[6] One may perhaps refer to the Roman *versura* (from *verto*—'to turn'), but unfortunately about this too only little is known; see M. Kaser, *Das römische Privatrecht*, i (1955), p. 414. [7] See p. 29, above.

yet having been repaid. But disputes may arise also with regard to the monthly payment of interest or some instalment on account of the capital; hence in C 11 the debtor stipulates that he is entitled to a receipt for any payment,[1] whether on account of the capital or on account of the interest. In case of complete discharge of the debt there was no need for a receipt; the return of the deed of loan would serve the same purpose. So, the fact that K 11 is part of the archive of Yehoyishma, the borrower's wife, shows that the debt was duly repaid.

An important matter in contracts of loan is the ensuring of repayment. Provisions for this purpose are contained in C 10 and K 11.[2] As for C 11, there is only the agreement about 'turning', just considered.

The first step with which K 11 threatens the defaulting debtor is the conversion of the debt from one of grain into one of silver. The debtor is to pay within twenty days of the non-discharge of the original obligation the sum of 1 karsh (= 10 shekels). This conversion of the debt is evidently of a penal nature, as is shown also by the use of the Persian term *'avigedan, the exact meaning of which is indeed not known, but which occurs regularly in penalty clauses. The ratio of the penalty cannot be ascertained, since we know nothing about the value of the grain due originally. Even though the money debt is penal, it seems that it supersedes the original obligation; in any case there is no further reference to the return of the spelt itself.

The next step, provided for in both C 10 and K 11, is the taking of pledges by the creditor.[3] The purpose of such distraint is not to give the creditor immediate satisfaction, but to put pressure on the defaulting debtor; i.e., the provision does not empower the creditor to collect the debt himself, without the debtor's consent, or, alternatively, without the intervention of the proper authority. This is clear also from the use of the term 'pledge' ('arevan) in both the documents.[4] The detailed list of items

---

[1] Cf. the provisions in Mishnah Baba Bathra 10. 6.
[2] Also in C 29 and 35, but not sufficiently preserved in either of these to be intelligible.   [3] Cf. p. 35, above.
[4] C 10: 9, 13, 17; K 11: 10. For the latter, cf. H. L. Ginsberg, JNES xviii (1959), pp. 148 f., R. Yaron, JNES xx (1961), pp. 127 f.

liable to be seized (C 10: 9 f.: ' . . . silver and gold, bronze and iron, male and female slave, barley, spelt, and any food . . .') seems also incommensurate with the satisfaction of a debt of 4 shekels, and rather appears as a means of making the debtor pay up (it is true that there is the possibility that the list is stereotyped, taken from the more substantial transactions). Both documents also provide that legal steps taken by the debtor against the seizure of pledges shall be of no avail. The provision is more express in C 10: 12 f.: 'and I shall not be able to complain against thee before governor or judge because thou hast taken pledges from me, while this document is in thy hand.' The production of the document will protect the creditor against a charge of unlawful distraint, which could occasionally have serious consequences.[1]

As already mentioned,[2] C 10 and K 11 contain also provisions in case of the death of the debtor. It is laid down that his heirs will be obliged to settle the debt, and the creditor's power to take pledges will be equally effective against them. On the other hand, we should mention that the Elephantine documents do not provide for any corporeal liability of either the debtor himself, or any of the members of his family.

No need is felt to state that in the event of the creditor's death, his claims would pass to his heirs. That is considered obvious.

II. *Lease*

The only Aramaic contract of lease, P. Meissner, has also some other claims to distinction. It is, for the time being, the oldest legal document in Aramaic, of 515 B.C., thus preceding C 1 by twenty years. Also, though its actual place of provenance is not known, scholars are agreed that it does not come from Elephantine. It has been discussed in considerable detail by A. Dupont-Sommer,[3] but is not yet fully understood. The difficulties are due, on the one hand to its poor state of preservation, on the other hand to the fact that it contains a number of terms not known from any other source.

---

[1] Cf. Laws of Eshnunna, secs. 22, 23, 24; Code of Hammurabi, secs. 114, 116.
[2] See pp. 41 f., 66, above.   [3] See p. 2, note 1, above.

The document, for a crop-sharing tenancy, is executed by the lessor. This is interesting, since the tenant is the party upon whom most of the obligations are imposed. Comparison with the demotic material shows that the practice was not uniform: some documents of lease are executed by the lessor (as here),[1] others by the lessee.[2]

The main provisions are as follows: the field is handed over for a period of one year, to be sown by the tenant with barley. Seed and work are to be provided by the tenant. The crop is to be divided between the two parties, each taking half. The share of the landlord is comparatively large, but there are parallels in demotic leases.[3] The lessor promises that he will not take away the field from the tenant, and in addition he undertakes to come to his defence in case of interference by a third party.[4] Beyond these provisions nothing is certain.

III. *Deposit*

Deposit is only cursorily referred to in the deed of 'removal' C 20, executed by the plaintiffs after litigation for the return of a variety of chattels ('garments of wool and cotton, vessels of bronze and iron, vessels of wood and ivory, corn and other things'), alleged to have been deposited by their grandfather with the father of the two defendants. The death of the original parties on both sides may have made it difficult to establish the facts. It seems likely that no written agreement accompanied the original transaction.[5]

[1] P. Louvre 7844, 7845, P. Loeb 45.
[2] e.g. P. British Museum 10432 (G. R. Hughes, *Saite Demotic Land Leases*, 1952, p. 9), P. Louvre 7836, 7839. Cf. also P. Murabba'at 24, a roll of extracts of leases, all drawn up from the point of view of the lessees.
[3] P. Louvre 7836, P. Loeb 45.
[4] See pp. 89 ff., above.
[5] See, however, p. 34 above, for the suggestion of Cowley and Pritsch, that the case was won by the plaintiffs. This, if correct, would render the assumptions made in the text superfluous.

IX

Some Problems of Comparison

OUR discussion has so far centred on the Aramaic documents themselves, their interpretation, and the examination of the legal notions underlying their various provisions. Such references to external sources as there have been, were made mainly in order to point out analogies. Having completed our survey of the documents and the spheres of legal activity with which they deal, we may now put the question as to the historical identity of the rules contained in them. This question is the more legitimate, as we are dealing with a group of documents from a small military garrison, remote from any centres of commerce and culture, and unlikely to have had an indigenous system of law, developed independently. However great their intrinsic value as evidence of ancient legal institutions and usage, the documents will gain in interest and importance if it is possible to establish, at least to some extent, their relationship to other systems of ancient law, earlier and later, within Egypt and outside it.[1]

We shall, in due course, turn to an examination of various systems which ought to be taken into account in a discussion of the historical sources of the Aramaic documents, and also such groups of documents as seem to bear the mark of contact with Elephantine or similar Aramaic material. But first of all, we wish to consider some principles generally relevant to a comparison of legal systems and the investigation of possible influences. We shall also point out some sources of error, hoping not to be misled by them. Needless to say, even less than in any other part of this book, shall we aim at an exhaustive treatment; we shall be satisfied with giving examples for our propositions.

[1] Cf. J. J. Rabinowitz, *Jewish Law. Its Influence on the Development of Legal Institutions*, 1956, and *Studies in Legal History*, 1958. For some criticisms of his work, see E. Volterra, *Iura*, viii (1957), pp. 546 ff., and R. Yaron, JSS vi (1959), pp. 308 ff.

I. *Similarity does not Imply Dependence*

The fact that two systems have arrived at an identical solution of a given problem in no way establishes either the direct dependence of one of the two upon the other, or their dependence upon a third source common to both of them. It is now common ground that similar economic and social conditions may lead to a similarity in legal institutions, even where any contact between two systems is out of the question. It follows that even if the circumstances do not rule out the possibility of contact, this still remains to be proved in each case.

K 5 evidences the existence, in Elephantine, of arrangements comparable to the Hellenistic παραμονή.[1] But the desire of a manumitter to retain some of the services of his former slave is a perfectly natural one, and arrangements of this kind are to be expected wherever there are slavery and manumission. Hence we should not be justified in claiming a connexion between the two institutions.

Another example is the clause, occurring both in C 15 and some Greco-Egyptian marriage contracts, which forbid a husband to alienate any property without the concurrence of the wife.[2] In this case there exists close substantive similarity. Some connexion between the Aramaic contract and the Greco-Egyptian ones is not ruled out, but it can nevertheless not be regarded as established.

In some cases it may be possible to advance farther. If, for example, we find that the position of women at Elephantine is one of considerable freedom, in excess of what is usual in the ancient Near East, but in agreement with their position in Egypt, it is reasonable to assume that Elephantine was influenced by Egyptian practice. Here the conclusion is supported by the overall picture.

We may then say that as far as rules of substantive law are concerned contact and influence should not be hastily suggested. One may be rather more confident when formal elements enter into consideration. True, defension clauses might well grow up

[1] See p. 39, above.   [2] See p. 52, above.

independently in different systems,[1] but when we find all of
them making use of verbs meaning 'to clean', this does prove
that they are somehow related to each other (though the details,
we shall see, may be very complicated).[2] Again, the notion of
'removal'[3] is so peculiar that its occurrence in Aramaic and
demotic documents is strongly suggestive of contact.

To establish contact and dependence, the similarity must be
such as would not be likely to arise independently. K 12 contains the phrase 'Yahu the God who dwelleth in Yeb the fortress'. Now the notion of a god who 'resteth', or 'dwelleth',
in a certain place is a very common one in early religion, to
be found as well, for example, in Babylonian, biblical, and
Egyptian sources. It will therefore in no way prove the influence
of any of these sources upon any other.

II. *The Time Factor in Comparison*

Where it is likely that provisions in two systems are not independent, the question arises which is the lender and which the
borrower, or indeed whether the two may not both be dependent upon some third source. Priority in time is a factor always
deserving of close attention. If it is very pronounced, that is to
say, if the feature in question appears very much earlier in one
system than the other, it can be regarded as decisive.

The notion of 'hate', in the context of divorce, is widely used
in Eastern sources, Hebrew *śane'* has this technical meaning in
a number of biblical texts.[4] Its Accadian equivalent, *zêru*, is in
general use already in Old-Babylonian times,[5] but is apparently
not known from Neo-Babylonian sources. We find it also in the
marriage contract from Alalakh (text 92), referred to above.[6]

---

[1] See pp. 89 ff., above.   [2] See pp. 117 ff., below.   [3] See pp. 81 f., above.

[4] Deuteronomy 24. 3, Judges 15. 2, Isaiah 60. 15; cf. Rabinowitz, p. 40; R.
Yaron, RIDA iv (1957), pp. 117 ff.; *śane'* is rendered 'to divorce' also in Malachi
2. 16, in the forthcoming *New English Bible* (as Professor Driver kindly informs
me).

[5] See, e.g., the series *ana ittišu* 7. 2. 49; Code of Hammurabi, sec. 142. Cf. Pritsch,
p. 15, note 7; P. Koschaker, ZA xxxv (1924), p. 200, note 2; M. San Nicolò,
Orientalistische Literaturzeitung, xxx (1927), col. 217; Driver and Miles, p. 292.

[6] See p. 48, above.

No marriage contracts from Ugarit have so far been published, and in a decree of divorce *ezēbu*—'to leave' (another term of divorce) is employed;[1] but we find *zêru* in a comparable context, the dissolution of adoption.[2] *zêru* occurs also in a Neo-Assyrian marriage contract, Nimrud 2307.[3] Evidently, then, 'to hate' is a technical term used widely over the ancient Near East in the sense of 'to desire separation'. Early Egyptian documents use other formulas for divorce, but 'to hate' (*mst*) does occur in demotic documents from late in the sixth century.[4] In this case two conclusions are warranted by priority in time: (*a*) the Aramaic documents are using Eastern terminology, (*b*) this Eastern terminology has been adopted by the Egyptians.

In the deeds of conveyance, the promise of non-interference with the alienee[5] contains detailed lists of active and passive parties. Comparison with lists in Neo-Assyrian, Neo-Babylonian, and Egyptian documents shows that the Aramaic lists are markedly different from the two former, but resemble closely the last-mentioned.[6] The earliest Egyptian source in which such a list of parties is given is apparently a legal stele from Karnak, of the seventeenth dynasty (eighteenth–seventeenth century B.C.).[7] About a century later there is the stele Cairo 34016,[8] then a document of the twelfth century,[9] finally there are the demotic documents of the Saite and Persian periods.[10] In this case it is clear that the Elephantine scribal practice is fashioned on Egyptian models.

But the situation is not always as simple as that. When the priority actually evidenced in the available material is of relatively small extent, it is difficult to arrive at a confident answer. One must take into account the possibility that priority may be

---

[1] Text 17. 159, PRU iv (1956), p. 126.
[2] Text 15. 92, PRU iii (1955), p. 54; text 16. 344, ibid., p. 75.
[3] Published by Barbara Parker, *Iraq*, xvi (1954), p. 37.
[4] For the first time in P. British Museum 10120A, of 517 B.C.
[5] See pp. 84 ff., above.
[6] See details in 'Conveyances', pp. 389 f.
[7] P. Lacau, *Une Stele juridique de Karnak*, 1949.
[8] P. Lacau, op. cit., p. 18.
[9] The 'Adoption Papyrus', see p. 49, note 3, above.
[10] e.g. P. Louvre 3228d (688 B.C.); P. Turin 246 (634 B.C.); P. Turin 248 (617 B.C.); P. Loeb 68 (502 B.C.).

only apparent, i.e. it may be due merely to accidents of transmission.

We have just referred to the notion of 'removal'. Within the Aramaic papyri it occurs first in C 6, of 465 B.C. It is to be found also in demotic documents, but does not go back to early Egyptian legal terminology. The phrase is first encountered in documents of the middle of the sixth century,[1] that is to say preceding the Aramaic documents by about a hundred years. The origin of the notion is in dispute: Th. Nöldeke[2] and Kraeling (p. 152) come out in favour of an Egyptian derivation; Kutscher (pp. 238, 244) and F. Rundgren[3] would prefer an Eastern solution. Here priority in time is not sufficient to be conclusive, and on the material available to us lender and borrower cannot be identified. There are in this case some further factors detracting from the force of demotic priority. Such additional factors are of importance in many cases. They may either confirm a prima facie priority or refute it:

C 8 is the only Aramaic deed of conveyance in which the clause promising non-interference says that no one, other than the alienee, has power over the plot conveyed.[5] The expression is paralleled in a large number of demotic documents, the earliest of which is P. Rylands 1, of 643 B.C. Here the priority of the latter (about 180 years) is supported by the fact that the formula is common in demotic sources and occurs only once in Aramaic; hence its derivation from demotic practice seems fairly probable.

Two of the latest of the Elephantine papyri, K 9 (404 B.C.) and K 10 (402 B.C.), close with the statement that 'this document is valid'.[6] I have not found anything similar in Egyptian sources, nor are there close parallels in cuneiform ones. On the other hand, a similar phrase occurs very frequently in Greek

---

[1] Restored in P. Rylands 4 (566 B.C.); actually existent in P. Cairo 50058 (540 B.C.); see Seidl, *Rechtsgeschichte*, pp. 25, 26.

[2] ZA xx (1907), p. 145.

[3] *Zeitschrift für die alttestamentliche Wissenschaft*, lxx (1958), pp. 209 ff.

[4] See pp. 121 f., below.

[5] See p. 86, above.

[6] See 'Conveyances', p. 393.

sources, for the first time in an oration of Demosthenes (35. 13), and then in P. Elephantine 1 (311 B.C.), the earliest extant Greco-Egyptian document. In the present case the priority in time of the Aramaic documents (less than 100 years) appears to be offset by the frequency of the expression in Greek usage and its extreme rarity in Aramaic. I would suggest, therefore, that the phrase is of Greek origin.[1]

With regard to the time factor, there is a further question to be considered. The phrases, notions, structures, &c., which we are comparing, are often separated from one another by considerable gaps in time, sometimes extending over many centuries. Is comparison here permissible from the point of view of method, and how reliable are the results obtained in such circumstances?

The answer will vary according to the general state and character of the sources used. Whenever they are fairly continuous and plentiful, as, for example, in Roman law, from the end of the Republic onwards, this justifies a fairly exacting attitude in comparison; consequently, results, whether positive or negative, will be more definite. Even if one allows for a degree of hibernation, the suggestion, for example, that an expression or clause in a Constitution of Justinian reflects a source of the early Republic, would be received with hesitation. To make it acceptable, it would have to be shown, either that the expression or clause had been in continuous common use, or, at least, that the early source in which it occurs was known at the time of Justinian.

The situation is very different where the sources of the ancient Near East or of ancient Egypt are concerned. In spite of epoch-making discoveries, the unknown is still of no less extent than the known. Only within the last thirty years or so has legal research gained access to material from places like Mari, Nuzi, Alalakh and Ugarit, to mention only the most

---

[1] Not immediately relevant is the occurrence of a similar phrase, *wehakkol šarir weqayyam*—'and all is valid and standing', in Talmudic sources. This is apparently a translation from the Greek; see already A. Gulak, *Das Urkundenwesen im Talmud*, 1935, pp. 26 f.

important. Even if it is true that a continued increase of our knowledge may be confidently expected, it is yet likely that there will
always remain considerable blanks, due to the lack of material.
One has to work with such sources as are available and may
compare them even if many links are missing, if, that is, the
similarity is such as to make contact prima facie likely. The
results will often be valid and illuminating, even though it is
admitted that the gaps in time detract from the force of a
conclusion.

The defension clause, centering on the notion of 'cleaning',
will illustrate our point. In demotic sources the earliest such
clause occurs in P. Rylands 1 (643 B.C.). The nearest earlier
source are the documents from Alalakh and Nuzi, preceding
P. Rylands 1 by some 800 years. Here it is necessary to postulate
some mediation as yet hidden from our eyes. The survival of the
defension clause at a date later than Alalakh and Nuzi is shown
also by its occurrence in Neo-Babylonian documents, from the
last two decades of the sixth century B.C. onwards. These are,
however, too late to be the source from which the Egyptians
borrowed; on the other hand, it is very unlikely that they reflect
Egyptian influence, for which there is, at that period of the
decline of Egyptian power, no evidence. As far as the Aramaic
documents are concerned it may, therefore, appear an open
question whether 'cleaning' is part of their Eastern legal heritage, brought into Egypt by the immigrants, or whether they
took it over from the Egyptian notarial style. However, there
is good reason for giving preference to the former alternative.[1]

Another example, less clear-cut perhaps, is the phrase 'thou
hast satisfied my heart'.[2] 'Satisfaction of the heart' has been described as a purely Egyptian concept,[3] as a typical Egyptian
phrase (Kraeling, p. 152). It is the expression which character-
izes the demotic *Geldbezahlungsurkunde* (acknowledgement of
receipt of purchase price). In point of fact, however, the
Egyptian phrase has noteworthy precursors in the ancient Near

---

[1] See p. 118, below.   [2] See p. 81, above.
[3] J. Leibovitch, *Bulletin de l'Institut d'Égypte*, xviii (1936), p. 25.

East.[1] On the other hand, in Egyptian legal terminology the phrase is a *novum*, occurring for the first time in P. Rylands 1,[2] not to be found in the earlier deeds of sale in 'abnormal' hieratic. Here there is a gap of a thousand years separating the various cuneiform sources from Saitic Egypt,[3] and yet this does not rule out the possibility of borrowing. For the Aramaic documents, however, there remains the uncertainty whether they employ the phrase as part of their Eastern stock, or are following demotic models.

It must be borne in mind, of course, that essentially such gaps are obstacles in the way to reliable conclusions, not short-cuts. While, when dealing with ancient Eastern systems, we may occasionally disregard gaps, assumptions of contact between sources distant in time from one another are provisional, and one must always be ready to revise one's results as drastically as may be necessary.

To illustrate this, let us take the provisions concerning a bigamous marriage of the husband. In a marriage contract from Nuzi it is laid down that the husband may neither marry another wife in the lifetime of the first, nor take a concubine.[4] Greco-Egyptian marriage contracts of the second and first centuries B.C. state that the husband is entitled neither to bring in another wife, nor to keep a concubine or boy.[5] On the basis of the close substantive similarity of the clauses, and in view of the fact that Greek marriage was essentially monogamous,[6] one might, if no further material were available, deduce that the Greco-Egyptian clause depends on the Accadian one in two of its

[1] e.g. in Susa, MDP xxii, no. 83; in Mari, text no. 84, in G. Boyer, *Archives royales de Mari*, viii (1958); in Alalakh, text 52, of the eighteenth century B.C. (see its discussion by S. E. Loewenstamm, *Bulletin of the Israel Exploration Society*, xx (1956), p. 15, note 14 [Hebrew]); in Old-Babylonian texts, UAZP nos. 86, 95, in the series ḪAR.ra = ḫubullu 2. 104.

[2] See Seidl, *Rechtsgeschichte*, p. 24.

[3] But note the distinctly legal meaning of 'and the priest's heart was satisfied', Judges 18. 20.

[4] Text 25, in C. H. Gordon, 'Nuzi Tablets Relating to Women' (see p. 60, note 4, above).

[5] P. Giessen 2 (173 B.C.), P. Genève 21 (second century B.C.), P. Tebtunis 104 (92 B.C.).

[6] See W. Erdmann, *Die Ehe in alten Griechenland*, 1934, pp. 87 ff.; differently H. J. Wolff, *Traditio*, ii (1944), p. 81, note 177.

provisions: with regard to the taking of another wife, and with regard to taking a concubine; the boy would be superadded. However, there are other sources available, and the assumption of dependence is demonstrably wrong (in part at least).[1] The Neo-Babylonian Nebuchadrezzar 101, the Aramaic C 15 and K 7, and the Greco-Egyptian P. Elephantine 1, all prohibit the taking of a second wife, but do not refer to a concubine. Since these documents would have to be the links between Nuzi and the documents of second-century Egypt, we must conclude that the concubine of the latter documents is independent of the concubine of the former one.

III. *Kinds of Contact*

Where the fact of contact is not itself in dispute, it still remains to distinguish between various kinds of contact, of very different legal significance. We may classify contacts and influences, in an ascending order of importance, as follows: one system may take over from another (*a*) everyday terms, (*b*) technical, legal terms, (*c*) schemata, that is the structure of the documents as a whole, or of clauses within a document, and (*d*) a notion or rule of substantive law. Language and law will occasionally meet. Indeed in a sense this meeting is unavoidable, since law employs the media of language to express itself. It is nevertheless desirable to distinguish, as far as that is practicable, between the legal and the linguistic aspects of influence. In any encounter between two civilizations, there is usually a much broader line of contact between the languages than between the legal systems. Hence, in transferring results from the one plane to the other one must make due allowance for the different intensity of possible influences.

(*a*) Contacts of a purely linguistic nature are basically devoid of legal interest and significance. To recognize them may be of help in the correct interpretation of a document, but that is all. We are here outside the sphere of law altogether. K 5 uses a Persian word, **āzāta*, for free.[2] Once we realize that the word is

---

[1] But see p. 127, below, for the main provision, concerning a second wife.
[2] See p. 38, above.

Persian, we shall no longer look for an explanation in Aramaic, and a possible source of error is eliminated. But, in the absence of proof, there is no ground for believing that the use of the Persian term has any legal significance, for example, that the freedom described by it differs in its nature from that which might have been described by the ordinary Hebrew or Aramaic terms.

K 7: 37–40 contains rather obscure provisions concerning the mutual behaviour of the spouses,[1] the interpretation of which turns on the meaning of the double negation 'not to be able not to do'. Ginsberg (p. 159) correctly interpreted the double negation as equal to an affirmation. There is, however, the difficulty that in Semitic languages a double negation is a negation emphasized, not an affirmation. This difficulty is satisfactorily disposed of once it is recognized that the phrase in K 7 is the translation of a demotic idiom.[2] However, this demotic idiom is essentially non-legal; hence, its transfer to Aramaic is devoid of legal import.

(b) More interesting for our purpose are linguistic influences of a decidedly legal flavour, the many instances where it is the style, the phrasing of legal documents, which is taken over by one system from another. However, here again the borrowing may be of greater or lesser significance.

We have referred to 'satisfaction of the heart'.[3] The use of the phrase in Egyptian documents may indicate that they are influenced, directly or indirectly, by the cuneiform documents in which a similar phrase occurs. It does not, however, prove the existence of a common legal notion as to the nature of such satisfaction and its consequences.

The phrase 'thou hast upon me' in deeds of loan, occurs in cuneiform sources, and in demotic and Aramaic documents.[4] This suggests borrowing or dependence on a common source,

---

[1] See p. 61, above.

[2] Cf. W. Spiegelberg, *Demotische Grammatik*, 1925, sec. 481: *Zwei Negationen verstärken eine positive Bedeutung.* As an example he quotes from P. Rylands 9 2/18: *bn 'w (= y) rḫ tm hb* = (literally) 'I shall not be able not to send' = 'I shall be compelled to send.'

[3] See p. 105, above.   [4] See p. 93, above.

but it does not imply an identical view of the nature of a debtor's obligation.

The phrase 'and no suit or process (shall obtain)' is frequent in the Aramaic papyri.[1] Equivalent phrases are common in early Eastern, demotic and Greco-Egyptian documents, as well as in Mishnaic Hebrew. This seems good evidence of contact between the various groups of documents, but it does not follow that there is substantive legal influence.

The phrase *kol yeraḥin ušenin* ('all the months and years') occurs in the very fragmentary C 45: 8. The details of the document are obscure, but it is clear that the passage containing the phrase refers to an undertaking to pay a sum of money or quantity of grain. In view of the lack of a context Cowley refrains from suggesting any interpretation. The Egyptian equivalent of the phrase, *ibd nb rnp. t nb*, occurs regularly in early deeds of loan.[2] The following is the promise of repayment in P. British Museum 10113: 3 ff.: 'I shall give it to thee in the year 21, month of Choïak. If I do not give it to thee in the year 21, month of Choïak, it will begin to bear interest, at the rate of $\frac{1}{3}$ a kite per deben silver per month, without interruption, during all the months all the years that it will remain with me.'[3] In effect the meaning then is that interest is due as long as the debt has not been paid. The Aramaic phrase is very probably translated from Egyptian legal terminology. This is good evidence of contact, but of no substantive legal import.

The situation is rather different with regard to 'cleaning', in the defension clause, to which we have referred repeatedly. Since in Egyptian documents the use of the typical verb is coeval with the clause itself, it is probable that the clause as a whole, of substantive legal import, was taken over from ancient Eastern sources.

---

[1] See p. 30, above.

[2] See, for example, P. British Museum 10113 (568 B.C.); P. Louvre 9293 (499 B.C.); P. Berlin 3110 (488 B.C.).

[3] The translation is an English rendering of that of M. Malinine, *Choix de textes juridiques en hiératique 'anormal' et en démotique*, i (1953), pp. 16 f. One change is made: on the analogy of the Aramaic phrase, it is suggested that *ibd nb rnp. t nb* is plural; hence 'all the months, &c.', not 'every month, &c.'.

(c) Similarities in the structure of documents are also evidence of contact between different systems. An examination of the schema of the Aramaic documents and its comparison with the schemata of Babylonian, Assyrian, and Egyptian documents, reveal basic differences from the two Eastern groups, and close similarities to the Egyptian one.[1] To mention just a few characteristic points: Aramaic and Egyptian documents are written in subjective style, as monologues, as a recital by the party executing the documents. The Eastern documents are in the main in objective style, and where subjectively styled, they are dialogue-documents (*Zwiegesprächsurkunden*),[2] embodying declarations of offer and acceptance. Aramaic and Egyptian documents are dated at the beginning, Eastern documents at the end. In Egypt the list of witnesses follows the name of the scribe by whom the document was written,[3] in Eastern documents the order is reversed. All this tends to show close contact between the Aramaic and Egyptian documents, at least in the field of structure.[4]

On the other hand we should mention the tripartite divorce clause. In two marriage contracts, C 15, K 7, the clauses concerning divorce consist of three parts: first, the hypothesis is put of a spouse divorcing the other spouse; second, the payments to be made in that event are laid down; third, it is provided that the wife will depart from the matrimonial home. The same tripartite divorce clause is to be found also in earlier Eastern sources. It appears in a marriage contract from Alalakh,[5] and also in a decree given by the Hittite Greatking, Tudḫalia IV, concerning the divorce of Ammistamru II, king of Ugarit, and his wife, the daughter of the king of Amurru.[6]

Then there is the so-called 'diagnosis-pattern', occurring in

---

[1] See 'Schema', pp. 55 ff.

[2] See M. San Nicolò, 'Zur Entwicklung der babylonischen Urkundenformen', *Festschrift Hanausek*, pp. 7 ff. of the reprint.

[3] Exceptions: P. Meissner, C 1, 11, 46; cf. p. 12, above.

[4] For some qualifications, see 'Schema', pp. 59 ff. On the relation of the Aramaic and demotic documents, see already Pritsch, p. 14, and L. Blau, *Festschrift Hermann Cohen*, 1912, pp. 209, 218.

[5] Text 92; see p. 48, note 4, above.

[6] Text 17. 159, PRU iv (1956), p. 126.

C 18 and K 7, both written by the same scribe, Ma'uziah b. Nathan.[1] These marriage contracts provide for certain possibilities; but instead of the usual simple conditional sentence, made up of an act or occurrence, in the protasis, and its consequences, in the apodosis, in these documents a definition of the act or its perpetrator is inserted in between. For example, in C 18: 3: 'If she says thus' (act), 'guilty she is' (definition), 'she will not be listened to' (consequence); K 7: 38 f.: 'And if thus he does not do unto her, divorce it is, he shall do unto her the law of divorce.' The scribe here makes use of a pattern apparently borrowed from biblical legislation. This tripartite pattern, (a) act, (b) definition of that act, or name given to its perpetrator, (c) consequences, occurs repeatedly in the Code of Holiness and also in other parts of the Priestly Source. The following two examples will suffice:

Leviticus 20: 14	And if a man take with his wife also her mother,	(act)
	wickedness it is (*zimmah hi'*),	(definition)
	they shall be burnt with fire both he and they.	(consequences)
Numbers 35: 17	And if he smote him with a stone in the hand,	
	whereby a man may die, and he died,	(act)
	a murderer he is (*roṣeaḥ hu'*)	(definition)
	the murderer shall surely be put to death.	(consequences)

There is reason to assume that the biblical 'diagnosis-pattern' is itself derived from other sources. D. Daube[2] has pointed to Egyptian and Babylonian medical codes, where the following arrangement is frequent: (a) symptoms, (b) diagnosis, (c) treatment. For example, the Edwin Smith Surgical Papyrus (a seventeenth-century B.C. copy of an earlier medical text) contains forty-eight items of this kind. The comparison gains in interest once one recalls the medical functions of the biblical

---

[1] See 'Marriage Contracts', pp. 34 f.
[2] *Abstracts of Proceedings of the Oxford Society of Historical Theology*, 1944–5, pp. 39–42.

priests; in this context also use is made of the same pattern.[1] In ancient legal sources the pattern occurs but rarely;[2] medicine is its obvious *Sitz im Leben*.

In spite of the other sources just mentioned, within the Aramaic documents the occurrence of the diagnosis-pattern ought to be regarded as a link with biblical legislation. The other legal sources are too remote in time, especially when one remembers that the pattern occurs in Elephantine only in two of the late documents (about 420 B.C.). A borrowing by the Elephantine scribe from Egyptian medical treatises is not likely; the difference in the subject-matter would be too great for him to bridge.

(*d*) Substantive contacts and influences are, of course, the most interesting, but also, where there are no formal elements to facilitate proof, difficult to establish; there is often the possibility of independent parallel development. We have already referred to some examples. I consider it not unlikely that the favourable position of women in Elephantine was due to Egyptian influence, even though I am not able to adduce any formal point which would support this view. I have also suggested that the demotic defension clause is an adaptation of the corresponding Eastern provisions, and in this case such a contention derives considerable support from the linguistic similarity, the use of verbs meaning 'to clean'. Again, under the impact of Eastern practices the monogamous nature of Greek marriage may have weakened: legal polygamy is implied by the clauses in some early Greco-Egyptian marriage contracts, specially prohibiting a bigamous marriage.[3]

---

[1] e.g. Leviticus 13. 3: '. . . and when the hair in the plague is turned white, and the plague in sight be deeper than the skin of his flesh, a plague of leprosy it is, and the priest shall look on him, and pronounce him unclean.' Cf. also G. v. Rad, *Theologische Literaturzeitung*, lxxvi (1951), cols. 129–32; R. Rendtdorff, *Die Gesetze in der Priesterschrift*, 1954, pp. 74 ff.

[2] Daube refers to the Code of Hammurabi, secs. 7, 9, 10, 11, and 13, where the perpetrator of certain acts is defined as thief (*šarrāqum*), or felon (*sarrum*), and his punishment is laid down. See also secs. 24, 26 of the Laws of Eshnunna; secs. 187, 188 of the Hittite laws, *in pari materia* with the Code of Holiness, define certain devious sexual behaviour as *ḫurkel*—'abomination', *Greuel* (at any rate, if one can rely on the translation from the Hittite).

[3] See p. 106, above; p. 127, below.

IV. *Proximate and Remote Influence*

Contacts and influences may be direct, immediate, proximate, or remote, indirect. In the context of Elephantine, when speaking of the former, we have in mind those examples which were before the eyes of the scribes who formulated the Aramaic deeds. In this sense a clause or phrase will be 'Egyptian' even if it can be proved that one step farther back the Egyptians themselves took it from somewhere else, say from Babylonian law; it will be 'Jewish' if it reached Elephantine via Jewish sources, whatever its ultimate historical origin (the diagnosis-pattern may be a case in point). It is on this direct influence that we must concentrate if our inquiry is not to become too complicated and too vague. A further point has to be taken into account: once a considerable time has passed, a foreign element may be so completely absorbed that it becomes part and parcel of the cultural property of the borrower nation. This would be equally possible in the spheres of language, law, and religion, to mention just a few obvious categories. If, after such a development has taken place, the receiving culture in turn exercises influence upon some third cultural entity, and in doing so passes on also what it itself had borrowed, the role of the original lender rather recedes into the background.

X

Sources and Contacts

So far we have formulated general propositions concerning comparison. We now turn to the various systems of law and groups of legal documents which have to be reckoned with as possibly exercising influence upon the Aramaic papyri. The main distinction we shall make will be between the law of the ancient Near East on the one hand, and Egyptian law on the other. We may say at the outset that the former will prove by far the more important factor.

'The law of the ancient Near East' is a convenient collective term, but one ought to be aware of its inexactitude: it embraces systems and traditions widely divergent from one another. To be sure, there is much that is common to all or most of them, but once one goes into details one will come across many basic differences. The use of the collective term is, however, justified by two main considerations. First, it will suffice for the purposes of an elementary study to indicate the general provenance of a phrase or notion, without aiming at more exact definition. Secondly, the gaps in the material available for comparison are very considerable; consequently, if a phrase or notion occurs in a particular source, say in documents from Nuzi, attributing it to that place will necessarily be haphazard, because the lack of evidence from other sources may be accidental. For instance, in discussing the 'divorce money' (*kesaf śin'ah*) stipulated in the marriage contracts,[1] we can point to parallels in Old-Babylonian texts,[2] and in Old-Assyrian texts from the Kültepe.[3] But we know that these both precede the Elephantine texts by at least 1,200 years and cannot therefore be a source of direct influence; hence, for our purpose, they become, vaguely perhaps and

---

[1] See pp. 56 ff., above.
[2] *uzubbūm*, in the Code of Hammurabi, sec. 139; in the series *ana ittišu*, 7.2.51, 7. 3.1; in UAZP 2 and 7; cf. Kraeling, p. 148.   [3] *ezibtu*, in EL 3 and 276.

inexactly, 'sources of the ancient Near East'. Only on certain limited matters shall we try to be more specific. In particular we shall try to separate 'Syrian' and biblical influences from the general Eastern mass.

We do not know whence the original Aramaic-speaking settlers came to Egypt and Elephantine. But bearing in mind the language of the documents and the national identity of most of the parties and scribes, one would naturally wish in the first instance to base one's comparison on documents written in Aramaic and Hebrew, originating from what we may call the 'Syrian' sphere, including all the inhabited areas along the Mediterranean coast, roughly from the present-day Turkish border to that of Egypt. However, we at once encounter an insurmountable obstacle: the only documents relating to private legal transactions comparable to the Elephantine material come from Alalakh and Ugarit, at the northernmost end of the area (and are written chiefly in Accadian). They are thus considerably remote in space, but no less aggravating is the remoteness in time. The latest of these documents, from Ugarit, are of the thirteenth century B.C., that is to say they precede Elephantine by about 800 years. Only some international treaties have survived in Aramaic, and these are not relevant to our discussion. No Phoenician legal document has come down to us, nor do we have any legal document from Israel or Judaea. There is, of course, the Bible, a source of the utmost importance for the study of ancient Eastern law, but none the less of a nature quite different from the Elephantine documents, the product of everyday legal activity. The first point then to bear in mind is the virtual absence of material from those sources which might be expected to be most directly relevant to our inquiry.

Clear contacts with the Bible (as distinct from 'Syrian' sources generally) are few and precarious. Cowley goes so far as to say that 'the Pentateuch, both in its historical and legal aspects, was unknown in the fifth century to the Jews of Elephantine'.[1] The open, undisguised taking of interest[2] speaks in favour of this view. On the other hand one can point to the 'diagnosis-

---

[1] Introduction, p. xxviii.　　　　[2] See p. 94, above.

pattern',[1] which establishes a clear link with biblical legislation. Less significant, but still noteworthy, is the phrase *beḥayyay uvemothi*—'in my life and at my death'.[2] This has a Biblical parallel in David's lament for Saul and Jonathan (2 Samuel 1. 23),[3] and is not known to me from any other Eastern source.

Some items of terminology are 'generally Syrian'. The phrase 'from today and for ever'[4] has close parallels in biblical texts,[5] but it has been shown to have antecedents in Alalakh and Ugarit.[6] Demotic parallels also exist,[7] but they are in this case rather late, and hence not likely to be the model for Elephantine.

The phrase 'and thy sons after thee'[8] emphasizes that a conveyance is not limited to the lifetime of the alienee. Once again, comparable phrases are common in biblical texts,[9] but we encounter similar expressions in conveyances from Ugarit: property is sold (or given as a gift) 'to X and his sons'.[10] I have found nothing exactly similar in Babylonian and Assyrian documents. In Egyptian documents the same idea of continuity is expressed differently: the rights are to pass from 'son to son, heir to heir'.[11]

We have here singled out as 'Syrian' items which do not occur in other ancient Eastern sources, and which may therefore be assumed to have originated within the Syrian sphere. There are other examples, which are generally Eastern, but with regard to which there is preserved evidence of Syrian mediation which accounts for their presence in Elephantine. The most obvious is the use of 'hate' as a term of divorce;[12] from Sumerian and Babylonian sources we see it pass to Alalakh, Ugarit, and the

---

[1] See pp. 110 ff., above.   [2] See p. 78, above.
[3] Pointed out already by L. Blau, *Magyar-Zsidó Szemlè*, xxv (1908), p. 254; cf. also *Gifts*, pp. 120 f.   [4] See pp. 47, 84 f., above.
[5] e.g. Isaiah 9. 6, 59. 21, Micah 4. 7, Psalms 113. 2.
[6] S. E. Loewenstamm, *Israel Exploration Journal*, vi (1956), p. 222.
[7] See P. Loeb 43 (525 B.C.), P. Bibliothèque Nationale 223 (516 B.C.), P. Louvre 7128 (511 B.C.).   [8] See pp. 65, 83, above.
[9] e.g. Genesis 17. 8, Joshua 14. 9; cf. Rabinowitz, pp. 129 f.
[10] See, for example, text 15. 37, PRU iii (1955), p. 35.
[11] e.g. in the Coptos Decree of Antef (of the 13th dynasty, eighteenth century B.C.) (see J. H. Breasted, *Ancient Records of Egypt*, i, secs. 778, 780), and in the Dakhle stele (22nd dynasty, tenth century B.C.), published by A. H. Gardiner, JEA xix (1933), p. 19.   [12] See pp. 101 f., above.

Bible, to find it finally in Elephantine, and also in demotic sources. Another instance is 'satisfaction of the heart', which occurs in documents from Alalakh, and in the Bible.[1] The payment of a brideprice, *mohar* in the Bible and at Elephantine, *terḫâtum* in the sources written in Accadian, may also be mentioned in the present context. The payment as such is, of course, extremely widespread, but Elephantine shares with Old-Babylonian texts and Alalakh even the peculiar feature of its being handed over to the bride.[2]

The antecedents of the defension clause are very complicated. The basic feature, common to a great variety of sources,[3] is the use of verbs meaning 'to clean': it is this notion which justifies the assumption of contact. It is, however, necessary to carry the investigation farther. In the Aramaic papyri the clause is made up of three verbs: to stand up, to clean, to give (back).[4] If we trace these components in the earlier sources, interesting results will emerge.

'To stand up' seems to have its root in a different clause altogether. In Old-Babylonian documents, and in documents from Susa, there is usually a warranty clause, providing that in case a claim is laid to the property, the alienor 'will stand up for the claim' (*ana baqri izzaz*); a variant, in Old-Babylonian texts, is 'he will answer for the claim' (*ana baqri ippal*).[5] When clauses of the *uzuzzu*-type meet with clauses of 'cleaning', a mixed formula might result, even if the original import of the two clauses was very different. Such a merger is to be found in some Susa documents: the seller *izzazma ubbeb*—'will stand up and clean'.[6] Followed by the more forceful 'to clean', 'to stand up' may have deteriorated to auxiliary status,[7] and probably no longer contributed anything material to the clause.

---

[1] See pp. 105 f., above. [2] See p. 48, above.

[3] See p. 90, above. [4] In K 1 *meqam*—'to stand up', is omitted.

[5] *uzuzzu* and *apālu* are generally understood as expressing the seller's responsibility in case of eviction (*Eviktionsklausel*), not a duty to defend the buyer. Rabinowitz, pp. 142 ff., argues in favour of the latter construction. It is a question which need not concern us here. Whatever the actual import, in form the two clauses are quite different.

[6] MDP xxii, texts 49, 79; cf. CAD iv, p. 7: 'Will be responsible for clearing'.

[7] See pp. 89 f., above.

The third component, 'to give (back), apparently only of secondary importance, is (like 'to stand up') to be found already in some Susa documents.[1] *zukku-nadānu* ('to clean—to give [back]') is very frequent in Nuzi,[2] but there are also many texts in which *nadānu* is dispensed with.[3] The Neo-Babylonian defension clause, occurring first in NRV 75, of 514 B.C., has *murruqu-nadānu* ('to clean—to give') as a constant, stereotyped combination.[4]

The different composition of the clause in the different documents enables us to distinguish three groups. There are those clauses which have only 'to clean'; so in the documents from the Kültepe,[5] from Alalakh,[6] and in the demotic sources.[7] None of these can have been the direct source of the Aramaic clause: one would have to assume, quite implausibly, that after borrowing 'to clean', for example, from the demotic, the Aramaic scribes added 'to stand' and 'to give' on their own initiative; but these are the very verbs which we have already found to occur in other sources. The double clauses, 'to clean—to give', look at first sight more promising. They begin in Susa, are frequent in Nuzi, and have become stereotyped in the Neo-Babylonian documents. But the two last-mentioned groups do not account for 'to stand up'. This must either have come down, through channels not yet discernible, the long way from Susa; or else the merger of 'to stand up' and 'to clean', which we have traced in the Susa documents, may have occurred also later in some other place where the warranty 'he will stand up for a claim' and that 'he will clean' happened to meet. Such meeting did not occur either in Nuzi or in the Neo-Babylonian documents. The final

---

[1] See MDP xxii, text 47, where the editor's restoration *izzaz*] *ubbeb inaddima* would give a formula very similar to that of the Aramaic papyri, but is not sufficiently reliable. The editor derives *inaddima* from *nadû*, and renders it *rejettera*. The correct derivation, there can be little doubt, is from *nadānu*; see also J. J. Rabinowitz, *Vetus Testamentum*, xi (1961), p. 72. In MDP xxiii, texts 320, 321, the combination *ubbubu-nadānu* refers to the action of judges: they cleaned and gave the object to the defendant.

[2] e.g. AASOR xvi (1936), texts 21, 34, 37, 42, 52, &c.

[3] e.g. ibid., texts 15, 16, 17, 18.   [4] e.g. NRV texts 75, 81, 83, 84, &c.

[5] *ubbubu*: EL 105, 205, 215, 216.   [6] *zukku*: Texts 66–70.

[7] *n'*: P. Rylands 1 (643 B.C.); Stele Florence 1639 (584 B.C.); P. Rylands 8 (560 B.C.); P. Loeb 68 (501 B.C.). *w'b*: P. Bibliothèque Nationale 223 (516 B.C.); P. Louvre 7128 (510 B.C.).

result then is that the immediate source from which the Aramaic defension clause is derived is not to be found in the material available, notwithstanding the fact that all clauses about 'cleaning' are in some way related to one another.

Several of the Elephantine conveyances give detailed descriptions of the house conveyed.[1] So, for example, K 10: 2: 'I have given thee a house. The construction of the lower storey has beams and three doors.' This may be compared with the descriptions usual in Neo-Assyrian documents: . . . *ein bebautes Hausgrundstück, nebst seinen Balken, nebst seinen Türen.*[2] The similarity between the two becomes more stressed when one compares the description occurring in Neo-Babylonian documents, which is quite different: . . . *ein bebautes Hausgrundstück,*[3] *festgemachte Türangelsteine, überdachtes Haus, Tür und Schloß sind befestigt.*[4]

The irrelevance of the Neo-Babylonian defension clause, and the difference in the description of houses are two items, unconnected and in themselves certainly not decisive, but pointing to a notable fact: there is, to my knowledge, in the Elephantine documents no evidence of contact with Neo-Babylonian legal sources. Wherever Neo-Babylonian practice or legal style strikes out on its own, differing in any way from earlier Eastern sources, we shall not find Elephantine in agreement with it. On the other hand, differences are many and basic: the schema of the documents is quite different; the 'dialogue-document', an important innovation in Neo-Babylonian legal style, has no parallel in Elephantine; penal stipulations are different, as are also the lists of parties; one could continue this list, but there is no need to do so. As the Neo-Babylonian material available for comparison is plentiful, there is for once little reason to fear that

---

[1] See 'Conveyances', p. 253.   [2] e.g. ARU, texts 341, 357, 359.
[3] San Nicolò (see the following footnote) renders *fertiges Haus*. The Accadian term *bītu epšu* is common to both the Neo-Assyrian and the Neo-Babylonian documents, and I have adjusted the translation to that of ARU. Which of the two renderings is preferable is here immaterial. Cf. also CAD iv, pp. 246 f.
[4] M. San Nicolò, *Babylonische Rechtsurkunden des ausgehenden 8. und des 7. Jahrhunderts v. Chr.*, 1951, texts 13, 16, 26, 30. This stereotyped phrase goes back to Old-Babylonian times; it occurs already in the series *ana ittišu*, 4. 3. 70–4. 4. 3, and in ḪAR.ra = ḫubullu, 2. 65–68.

our conclusions will be invalidated by new discoveries; nor is it likely that new documents from Elephantine would change the picture considerably. We may then assert that the Aramaic legal style, whether in Egypt or outside it, had reached the phase observable in the Elephantine documents before Neo-Babylonian influence could make itself felt. Its Eastern contacts apparently date from considerably earlier times. Two possible exceptions are the description of house-property (just considered), which probably depends on Neo-Assyrian models, and the biblical diagnosis-pattern, used in Elephantine late in the fifth century.[1] Both have nothing to do with the Neo-Babylonian documents. We cannot, therefore, accept Kraeling's suggestion (at pp. 49 f.) that Babylonian influences evidenced in the Elephantine documents are a consequence of the Persian conquest of Egypt (525 B.C.), which introduced into Egypt a bureaucracy 'used to the Babylonian way of doing things'.

In view of what has just been said it will not surprise the reader that instances of Persian influence are also very few and of little importance. We know next to nothing about Persian substantive law, or Persian notarial practice, but they are unlikely to be of much significance in evaluating the Elephantine material;[2] this contains little that cannot be explained in terms of Eastern or Egyptian law. The Persian mark on Elephantine is limited to a few isolated items of terminology. Already early in the fifth century, in the first of Cowley's documents, we find the dry measure *ardab (C 2), and the unit of weight of silver *karsh (already in C 1); measures and units of silver migrate very easily and no legal significance need attach to their doing so.[3] All other Persian terms occur only in the last quarter of the fifth century, that is to say after a hundred years of Persian rule.[4] We may mention the use of terms designating certain relatives

---

[1] See pp. 110 ff., above.   [2] Cf. Kutscher, p. 247.

[3] The same applies also to the occurrence of the Greek *stater* in some of the latest Elephantine documents (C 35, 37, K 12).

[4] For a discussion of these Persian influences see I. Sheftelowitz, *Scripta Universitatis atque Bibliothecae Hierosolymitanarum*, I/iv (1923), who deals with all the material then available. See also the reviews of the Brooklyn papyri by J. de Menasce (*Bibliotheca Orientalis*, xi (1954), p. 161), E. Benveniste (*Journal Asiatique*, vol. 242 (1954), p. 298), W. Eilers (*Archiv für Orientforschung*, xvii (1956), p. 333).

of parties; these are *hangith, *hanbag, and *'adrang.[1] The earliest dated document in which any of them occurs is K 5, of 427 B.C. It is there also that we have the word *āzāta—'free', which has already been mentioned.[2] *'avigedan—'penalty', occurs in several of the later documents, for the first time in C 20 and K 6, both of 420 B.C. Also for the first time in C 20 there is the military title *fratarak; the title *hapaṭhapta occurs in K 8, of 416 B.C. Another military term is *pathefa—'ration'.[3]

Having completed our brief survey of the relevant sources from outside Egypt, we may now consider the contacts of the Elephantine material with Egyptian law and practice. To begin with, there are straightforward cases where items of terminology to be compared are found already in early Egyptian sources: where Elephantine is in agreement with these (and where, we ought to add, there is no comparable Eastern material) it may be assumed that the Aramaic documents draw on the Egyptian model. We have already mentioned the Aramaic lists of parties, closely resembling the Egyptian ones;[4] also the provision that a complaint 'will not be listened to'.[5] These have close parallels already in the seventeenth-century stele from Karnak. The general resemblance of the schema of the Aramaic documents to that of the Egyptian ones, also already stressed,[6] is of particular importance.

Other instances, however, are more complicated. In the middle of the seventh century B.C. there occurs a break in the continuity of the Egyptian notarial style. With P. Rylands 1 a new script, demotic, comes into use, but innovations are not restricted to that. The demotic document has indeed a basic schema in common with the earlier hieratic one,[7] and takes over not inconsiderable portions of hieratic terminology (so, for example, those just mentioned as instances of Egyptian influence upon the Aramaic papyri); but there are far-reaching changes, in substance as well as in terminology. The existence of

---

[1] See 'Conveyances', p. 265.   [2] See p. 38, above.
[3] In K 11 (402 B.C.), C 43 (date not preserved), and in the non-legal C 24 (of 419 B.C.?).   [4] See p. 102, above.   [5] See p. 30, above.
[6] See p. 110, above.   [7] See Seidl, *Rechtsgeschichte*, p. 17.

this break in Egyptian legal development is, of course, well
known, but I am not aware of any satisfactory explanation for
it (nor am I competent to try to offer one here). It cannot be
our aim to go here into the many differences between the hieratic
and the demotic documents; Seidl discusses a considerable
number of them in the course of his book. As examples of items
as yet not found in pre-demotic Egyptian sources we might
mention the defension clause, the clause concerning the return
to the status quo ante (= *'*appam*-clause),[1] and 'satisfaction of
the heart', all three of which occur for the first time in P. Rylands 1. Considerably later is the notion of 'removal',[2] which
makes its appearance for the first time in P. Rylands 4, of
566 B.C. It is indeed not impossible that one or the other may
still turn up in earlier Egyptian texts: the stele from Karnak,
the terminology of which is in some respects without parallel
in early Egyptian law, serves as a salutary reminder how pre-
cariously dependent we are upon the accidents of transmission.
Yet, while this is a possibility to be borne in mind, its occurrence
is not very likely, and we may consider the matter on the basis
of the evidence now available.

As is well known, the emergence of the demotic document
follows shortly upon the brief period of Assyrian domination of
Egypt (671–663 B.C.). But in view of what I remarked above
about the slight impact of the prolonged Persian rule, I am unwilling to attach much importance to the Assyrian interlude,
especially since there is in the demotic material nothing suggestive of contact with the Neo-Assyrian documents. By contrast,
it is not insignificant that of the three items adduced from P.
Rylands 1, two are due to Eastern influence: certainly the defension clause, not improbably 'satisfaction of the heart'. I do not,
however, wish to imply that the reform of the Egyptian notarial
style was altogether the outcome of Eastern influence: there are
no apparent Eastern parallels for 'return to the status quo ante'
and 'removal', and it would be rash to argue that because Eastern
influence appears to be established on one point, one may postulate it with regard to others. The question must remain open.

---

[1] See p. 88, above.   [2] See pp. 81 f., 103, above.

How does all this affect the Aramaic papyri? The sudden emergence of the demotic document does not make it altogether impossible that the Aramaic documents may, with regard to some of the points mentioned, have been fashioned upon demotic models, but there is room for reasonable doubt. Where there is no evidence for Eastern influence upon the demotic terminology ('return to the status quo ante' and 'removal'), we may for the time being accept that the Aramaic documents follow the demotic. Where the demotic style is itself dependent on the East ('cleaning' and 'satisfaction of the heart'), one will be inclined to assume direct Eastern-Aramaic filiation, in view of the general ties of the two groups of documents. With regard to 'cleaning' other data have already enabled us to establish the Eastern origin of the Aramaic clause; this cannot be derived from the demotic,[1] in spite of the latter's priority in time, of about 130 years, separating P. Meissner from P. Rylands 1. 'Satisfaction of the heart' occurs first in C 6 (of 465 B.C.), that is to say demotic priority amounts in this case to 180 years. There would thus have been ample time for this phrase to have reached the Aramaic papyri by way of the demotic documents, and not directly from the East.

Much will also depend upon the question, just how early the use of Aramaic documents in Egypt began, and how widespread it was; again no answer can be given. Since 'cleaning' and 'satisfaction of the heart' are both of Eastern origin, possibly they were brought into Egypt by very early Aramaic documents, and the demotic followed the Aramaic.[2] With regard to 'cleaning' there is, of course, the difference between the tripartite Aramaic clause and the simple Egyptian one to be taken into account, and one would have to assume that the demotic scribes dispensed with the unessential 'to stand up' and 'to give'. The whole question is not yet capable of a reliable conclusion, and I prefer to leave the matter open.

The point primarily in issue with regard to 'satisfaction of the

[1] See p. 118, above.
[2] So Kutscher, with regard to 'cleaning' (see pp. 247 f.), but Seidl, in the last sentence of his *Rechtsgeschichte*, categorically rejects the possibility that the Aramaic documents may have introduced Eastern law into Egypt.

heart' is, as we saw, whether the direct influence upon the
Aramaic documents was Eastern or demotic. I suggested that
the Egyptians themselves were probably drawing on the East,
in other words that Elephantine was at least indirectly under
Eastern influence. There are other cases where we have to
decide between the East and Egypt as the source behind the
Aramaic documents, namely, where the East and Egypt are
apparently independent of one another, yet there is close
similarity. If in such cases an item in the Elephantine documents
agrees with both, there must always remain a degree of uncertainty as to its origin.

The deeds of sale expressly confer upon the buyer the power
of subsequent alienation: 'to whom thou desirest thou wilt give
it.'[1] The phrase has a long history in the East; it appears in the
Code of Hammurabi, and in documents from Susa and Nuzi.[2]
Originally the phrase was longer, and was used to confer a
limited power of appointment; for example: 'to whom *of my
sons* that thou desirest thou wilt give it.' Omission of the quali-
fying words (here in italics), at first perhaps for the sake of
brevity, gradually gave the clause a wider import.[3] Both the
stages of the phrases can be observed in Egypt too. In P. Kahun
I. 1 (of the twelfth dynasty, roughly contemporary with the Susa
documents), the wife is given a limited power of appointment
to the property of her husband: 'she shall give it to any she
desires of her children that she bears (has borne?) me.' In
P. Turin 2021 (20th dynasty, twelfth century B.C.) there is the
shorter phrase, in this case clearly referring to full power of
alienation.[4] In view of the evidence as a whole, Eastern derivation of the phrase which we find at Elephantine is very probable, but the Egyptian sources introduce a modicum of doubt.

The Aramaic deeds of sale are drawn up from the point of
view of the seller: he has given, or sold and given. It is typical

[1] See p. 83, above.

[2] See the various nuances in the Code of Hammurabi, secs. 150, 179; MDP
xxii, text 131, MDP xxiv, texts 378, 379, 382b; for Nuzi see AASOR x (1930),
texts 5, 20, 22, 24.

[3] See the discussion by Rabinowitz, pp. 17 ff. Cf. also Jeremiah 27.5: God, *creator
mundi* (and therefore its owner), disposes of it as he sees fit.

[4] Cf. Seidl, *Einführung*, p. 46.

of Egyptian formulary style, for many centuries prior to the Aramaic papyri, that deeds of sale are drawn up *ex latere venditoris*. In cuneiform documents formulation from the point of view of the buyer is prevalent, e.g. in Old-Babylonian documents,[1] in Susa,[2] Mari,[3] Alalakh,[4] and in Neo-Assyrian documents.[5] Not 'X has sold', but 'Y has bought'; strictly speaking, these are not deeds of sale, but deeds of purchase. However, this is only the general picture; on a more detailed inspection we find texts from various Eastern sources which differ from it. In a number of documents from Susa,[6] and from the Kültepe,[7] and in Middle-Assyrian documents[8] we find a double formulation, taking into account both the seller and the buyer: 'X has given (object) for a price, Y for (sum of silver) has bought', or the like. Two documents from Susa are drawn up solely from the point of view of the seller. 'X to Y has sold'.[9] More directly relevant to Elephantine, because closer in time and place, are the documents from Ugarit. There both the forms occur: some documents speak of purchase ('Y has acquired'), others of sale ('X has sold', or 'X has given').[10] The Neo-Babylonian documents have, as a rule, purchase of immoveables,[11] but always sale of moveables;[12] finally, in the time of the Seleucids, the latter form prevails and is used for both moveables and immoveables.[13] To sum up: the Aramaic deeds of sale, in being drawn up from the point of view of the seller, are in full correspondence with long-established Egyptian practice; it is nevertheless quite possible that they preserve Eastern (or 'Syrian') usage, say, the usage met with in part of the documents from Ugarit.

---

[1] e.g. UAZP 79, 80, 81, 86, 87, 88, &c.   [2] e.g. MDP xxii, texts 42, 43, 44, 45, &c.

[3] *Archives royales de Mari*, viii (1958), texts 2, 3, 4, 5, 9, 10.

[4] e.g. texts 62, 65, 66.   [5] e.g. ARU 337, 340, 341, 345, &c.

[6] MDP xxii, texts 52, 71–76.

[7] EL 105, 189; also TC iii. 253, published by J. Lewy, *Archives d'histoire du droit Oriental*, i (1937), pp. 102 ff.

[8] e.g. KAJ 149, 153, 170, P. Koschaker, *Neue keilschriftliche Rechtsurkunden aus der El-Amarna-Zeit*, 1928, pp. 149 ff.   [9] MDP xxii, text 41; MDP xxiv, text 361.

[10] See J. Nougayrol, PRU iii (1955), p. 27; cf. texts 15. 119 (p. 86), 15. 156 (p. 121), 16. 131 (p. 138).

[11] e.g. NRV 33, 34, 39, 40.   [12] e.g. NRV 63, 64, 65, &c.

[13] See M. San Nicolò, *Die Schlußklauseln der altbabylonischen Kauf- und Tauschverträge*, 1922, pp. 26 ff.; NRV, pp. 46 f., 91 f. H. Petschow, *Die neubabylonischen Kaufformulare*, 1939, pp. 3 ff.

The problem of Greek influence on the Elephantine papyri is difficult to answer with confidence. I have noted above that the final clause in K 9 and 10 ('this document is valid') may be of Greek origin;[1] but I am far from categorical on this point. There have been other suggestions of Greek influence of a linguistic nature, but they fail to carry conviction. We have already mentioned the reference to Greek money in some of the latest documents, and have denied it to be of any significance for the law.[2]

This brings us generally to the question whether there was any relationship between the Aramaic papyri of Elephantine (or Aramaic material of other places of provenance) and Greco-Egyptian documents. It has been suggested that Greco-Egyptian scribes adopted significant parts of the demotic formulary style, and that substantive Egyptian rules have also found their way into Greco-Egyptian practice.[3] If that is correct, then in this manner Eastern (and Aramaic) influences might pass from the demotic to the Greek documents. But we are here concerned with direct influence only, and this was necessarily limited in scope, since, it seems, Aramaic ceased to be used for the writing of documents not long after the Greek conquest of Egypt. Wherever a clause or phrase occurs in Aramaic, demotic and Greek documents, it is submitted that the Greek is more likely to have borrowed from the demotic, simply because the contact between these two was much broader (and this quite apart from the question whether in a given case the demotic or the Aramaic is the original). For example, the phrase 'and no suit or process',[4] found (apart from earlier Eastern sources) in Elephantine, in demotic and Greek documents, should not be put down to any direct Aramaic-Greek contact. The same holds true for the Neo-Assyrian description of houses:[5] when found in Greek documents,[6] they are best accounted for as loans from demotic.[7] One could add further examples of this kind.

---

[1] See pp. 103 f., above.   [2] See p. 120, above.
[3] R. Taubenschlag, *The Law of Greco-Roman Egypt in the Light of the Papyri*, 2nd ed. (1955), pp. 23 ff.   [4] See pp. 30, 109, above.   [5] See p. 119, above.
[6] See, for example, P. Amherst 51 (88 B.C.).
[7] See, for example, P. British Museum 10750 (213 B.C.), published by H. S.

This does not, however, preclude the possibility of direct Aramaic-Greek filiation. There is at least one relevant example: we have already mentioned that the clause in C 15 and K 7, forbidding a bigamous marriage, has close parallels in early Greco-Egyptian marriage contracts, starting with P. Elephantine 1 (311 B.C.). There are no comparable demotic provisions; early Eastern parallels (from the Kültepe, from Nuzi, and a Neo-Babylonian document) are too remote in time and space to compete effectively with the Elephantine documents as sources of direct influence.[1]

There remains a last point to be considered: is there any connexion between the Aramaic papyri and later Jewish sources, that is the Talmudic literature and the legal documents from the Judaean desert?[2] A qualifiedly affirmative answer can be given, insofar as both contain common Eastern legal heritage, but even that is rather limited. There are some items of terminology: the phrase 'in life and in death' has Talmudic parallels,[3] though it is found also in the Bible;[4] a phrase reminiscent of 'no suit or process' occurs in the Mishnah;[5] 'to hate' functions as a term of divorce in an isolated Talmudic dictum.[6] All these have already been pointed out by various scholars, who were often inclined to give too much weight to these correspondences. The treatment of the marriage contracts and their harmonization with the Talmudic *kethubah* were also very uncritical.[7] When one looks for items in which Elephantine and

Smith, JEA xliv (1958), p. 86. The demotic P. Rylands 17 (118 B.C.) contains the description also in Greek, in a receipt for taxes attached to it.

[1] Rabinowitz (pp. 43 ff.) has already pointed to the Elephantine documents as the source of the Greek provision, and I follow him in this instance; see also H. C. Youtie, JEA xl (1954), p. 114, note 4. Volterra, *Iura*, viii (1957), p. 555, holds that the similarity is due to Greek influence. However, about 440 B.C. (C 15) is too early a date for this to be acceptable.

[2] R. de Vaux, J. T. Milik, P. Benoit, *Discoveries in the Judaean Desert*, ii, 1961; see also *Revue Biblique*, lxi (1954), pp. 182 ff., *Biblica*, xxxviii (1957), pp. 255 ff. Our submissions will have to be re-examined in the light of further documents, which await publication.

[3] Mishnah Kethuboth 9. 1, Baba Qamma 9. 10; Babylonian Talmud, Baba Bathra 153a.   [4] See p. 116, above.

[5] Mishnah Kethuboth 9. 1.

[6] Palestinian Talmud, Kethuboth 30b, Baba Bathra 16c; cf. pp. 101 f., above.

[7] See p. 44, above.

the Talmud are exclusive partners, the results are very meagre. The phrase 'the witnesses are within' (*śahadayya' bego*)[1] may be an instance; possibly there are a few others of equally limited legal interest. On the other hand it is significant that various technical terms, which occupy a central place in the Elephantine documents, are missing in the later sources. They are missing even where the substance is similar; their place is taken by synonyms or near-synonyms. To mention some striking instances: instead of *reḥaq*—'to remove',[2] the Talmud has *silleq*;[3] *šalliṭ*—'to have power',[4] has been largely superseded by *reši*;[5] *naqqi* and **paṣṣel* of the defension clauses[6] have made place for *mareq* and *šappi*.[7] This means that, although there is some relationship between Elephantine and the sources of the Talmudic period— they may, for instance, be following common prototypes—there is no direct line leading from the former to the latter. This will not surprise when one recalls that the Elephantine documents and the Talmud are the products of different times and different countries.

[1] See p. 16, above.   [2] See p. 81, above.
[3] Babylonian Talmud, Baba Bathra 43*a*, and parallels.
[4] See pp. 72, 82, above.   [5] P. Murabba'at 26; cf. P. Murabba'at 19.
[6] See p. 90, above.
[7] See the Judaean deed of sale published by J. T. Milik in *Biblica*, xxxviii (1957), pp. 255 ff., P. Murabba'at 26, 30; in the Babylonian Talmud, see Baba Meṣi'a 15*a*.

INDEX OF AUTHORS

INDEX OF SOURCES

A. Sources in Aramaic; B. Biblical Sources; C. Post-biblical Jewish Sources; D. The Ancient Near East; E. Egypt; F. Greek and Roman Sources.

PRINTED IN GREAT BRITAIN
AT THE UNIVERSITY PRESS, OXFORD
BY VIVIAN RIDLER
PRINTER TO THE UNIVERSITY